PENNY CANDY, BOBSKATES *and* FROZEN ROADAPPLES

Growing Up in the Thirties & Forties

ROBERT H. THOMPSON

Orca Book Publishers

Canadian Cataloguing in Publication Data

Thompson, Robert H., 1923-
    Penny candy, bobstakes and frozen roadapples

ISBN 0-920501-39-7

    1. Thompson, Robert H., 1923-   2.
Saskatchewan — Biography. I. Title
FC3524.1.T48A3 1990   971.24'02'092
F1072.T48A3 1990   C90-091120-4

Publication assistance provided by the Canada Council.

Orca Book Publishers Ltd.
P.O. Box 5626, Stn. B
Victoria, B.C., Canada
V8R 6S4

Cover design by Susan Fergusson
Typeset by University of Victoria Students' Society Graphics Shop
Printed in Canada

Dedicated to the memory of my friends,
who gave their lives so that we may live in freedom.
"Too young . . . too young . . . much too young."

For Monte, Rick and Leanne, with love from Dad.
For Harley, Jesse, Kayla and Amber, with love from Grampa.
And for Doris, with love from her husband.

Contents

Prologue

Everyone has a hometown. Maybe it was no more than one grain elevator and a general store. For many, "hometown" was a large metropolitan centre like Vancouver or Toronto. Quite often, the place is not as important as the memories, because the place is going to change, sometimes beyond recognition, but the memories hold true and grow fonder with the passing years.

I hope that, when I talk about people you have never met, and refer to places you have never been, you will be able to relate my comments to people and places dear to you. For these are the reminiscences of a lad who grew up through the depression and the war, during a time the likes of which will never be seen again.

My hometown was Saskatoon, in the middle of the vast Canadian prairie. It is a city known for its treed parks and boulevards, its beautifully landscaped riverbank, and its interesting bridges. But its most important asset is its people, with their indomitable spirit and great civic pride. They are cut of the same cloth, two and three generations removed, as those Saskatonians who had the courage to publicly fund a new indoor ice rink at the height of the Great Depression.

What I miss most of all about my hometown are the four distinctive seasons of the year. Spring on the prairies comes as a welcome relief from the bitter cold, with showers that nurture a new mantle of green, and flowers that poke through from their winter hibernation. Summer follows, with trees covered in new growth; hot days and nights without respite, and fields of golden grain. Then comes the spectacular fall with its multitude of colours as poplar, maple and elm turn their leaves to hues of yellow, orange and flaming red. Winter has its own special beauty. Intricate patterns of sculpted snow; the crunching sound of its crispness underfoot, and the haunting whistle of a train carried through the night air; clear sunlit days and moonlit nights, and the beauty of frosted windows and snow-laden trees.

All in all it was certainly a wonderful place to grow up. And, in my particular case at least, the old adage holds true: "You can take a boy out of the prairies, but you can never take the prairies out of the boy."

Setting the Stage

If you were a kid growing up during the 1930's, you were lucky. I know — I was one of them. Granted, to many people today that may seem a funny thing to say given the fact that it was the era of the Great Depression. It's true that many fathers were out of work, and many families hard up. But as a result of all this kids were left pretty much on their own. We were left to amuse ourselves, to find our own entertainment. We didn't have TV and video games — some didn't even have a radio.

So what did we do? Well, we made up the neatest games and built the greatest playthings, and had more fun than you can shake a stick at. Perhaps we had more fun than any generation since! We had games like *Kick-the-can* and *Aunty-I-Over*, and we made things like kites and stilts. In the winter we built bobsleds and in the summer soap boxes. Girls played *Hop Scotch*, jacks and skipped rope. Boys had arrow guns and rubber band guns and sling shots, all handmade. When we played road hockey we wrapped magazines around our legs as shinguards, and used frozen horse manure, known as "roadapples," for pucks. We were free spirits, children of the Depression, doing our own thing. But more of all that later . . . I'm getting ahead of myself.

My dad had served overseas for the entire First War with the Saskatchewan Light Horse, an artillery regiment from Prince Albert attached to the 1st Canadian Division. He survived a German mustard gas attack, and following the battle was awarded the Order of the British Empire for gallantry. The medal was presented to him by King George V at an investiture at Buckingham Palace. One of the London newspapers carried a large photo of Mother and Dad leaving the palace — Dad in full dress uniform with medals; Mother in a long, black outfit with a silver fox stole and a fashionable hat. Later Dad also received the Oak Leaf Cluster for being mentioned in dispatches.

He kept a diary during his service in France, much of it simply relating to unit business and army friends. But it also included some humourous incidents, such as, "Last night a cow kicked over a tent peg and the front end collapsed . . . the tent's, not the cow's." One of the things that interested me was that in the entire set of diaries his strongest expletive was "those damned Boche." I suspect that Dad would not have approved of my somewhat superfluous use of more colourful language.

Dad had been a collector of war memorabilia, including a Lee Enfield and a Ross rifle, a German Luger, .45 and .38 handguns, several varieties of grenades, and a gas mask of the type used early in the war. This consisted entirely of a piece of khaki cloth with a celluloid eye shield that tied behind the head. It didn't appear to be effective enough to ward off the common cold, let alone protect against lethal quantities of mustard gas. Fortunately, more sophisticated masks with charcoal filters were developed later on.

One of the more interesting instruments of war in Dad's collection was a steel dart. It was one of hundreds that were dropped over the trenches from low flying aircraft. As it twirled towards the ground it picked up sufficient thrust to pierce a steel helmet. (Man has always come up with ingenious methods of getting rid of one another in wartime.) He also had a piece of aluminum from a German dirigible shot down over London, and a Gurkha's kukri knife stained with blood. It was part of the religious belief of these fierce fighters that, when the knife was drawn from its sheath in battle, it must taste blood before being returned.

Early photographs of mother show a petite, pretty lady with the stylish "wasp waist" of the times. She had been a young teacher for three years in Humboldt when she was wooed by a handsome army officer ten years her senior. They were married in St. John's Anglican Church,

and Frozen Roadapples

Lloydminster, on May 14, 1908. The newspaper coverage of their wedding included, in accordance with the custom of the times, a list of wedding presents and the donors' names. (Thank goodness that custom was done away with before too long. In the lean years, our wedding gifts fell into the category, "It's not the gift, but the thought that counts." Our "Bud vase, Mr. and Mrs. R. Thompson," wasn't something we would have wanted published in the newspaper.)

Prior to the war Dad had been a successful businessman and had owned the first automobile, a 1905 Ford, in Lloydminster. As a matter of fact, when my mother volunteered to do nurse's aide duty in England in order to be with Dad, she had an English nanny with her on the voyage over to help look after my older siblings, Pat and Bertie, who were two and five respectively. Poor health in the five years that preceded his death had pretty well depleted the family's assets.

Following the war Dad tried his hand, with varying degrees of success, in a number of businesses: owner of a real estate agency, partner in a lumberyard, an official for the Land Settlement Office, and editor of the Oliver, B.C. *Times*. At one time he had been appointed by the federal government to host an official party that came to Canada from Turkey to go duck hunting in Saskatchewan. As a "thank you" for his services he was presented with a large tapestry embroidered by the harem of the Turkish potentate. The needlework was so expertly done that it is impossible to tell one side from the other.

My father's health was never good after he returned from his service overseas and he died in April, 1923. I was born six weeks later, on June 1st. At the time of his death Dad was manager of the Community Lumber Company in Oliver. Shortly after his funeral the family moved to Richlea, Saskatchewan, to stay with my mother's parents, John and Elizabeth Lyons.

In 1925 our family moved to Saskatoon to live in a house on Main Street owned by my grandparents. My widowed mother was forty years old, my brother Bert was fourteen and my sister Pat was ten. The family lived in that house for the better part of thirty-five years, until Mother found it necessary to enter the Sunnyside Nursing Home where she spent the last ten years of her life. She died in 1977 in her ninety-second year. Bert served overseas for six years with the Saskatoon Light Infantry, 1st

Penny Candy, Bobskates

Division, and in the 1950s became their commanding officer. Pat was recently widowed and lives in a highrise near the Bessborough Hotel.

Grandpa Lyons was born in 1857 in New Boyne, Ontario, and at the age of nineteen had decided to follow Horace Greely's advice to "Go west, young man, go west." His parents tried to discourage him, reminding their son that the rebel, Louis Riel, was causing a lot of trouble in the Prairies, and was responsible for the murder of Thomas Scott in Fort Garry, where the young Lyons was headed. Undeterred he started out. His route took him through Chicago, Illinois, into the state of Minnesota and, finally up the Red River by tugboat to Fort Barry, Manitoba. Working for the railway he earned enough money to settle down, and on March 29, 1881, he married Elizabeth Williams during the worst blizzard Fort Garry had ever seen. "The snowdrifts were as high as mountains," he once told me, "but I started out for the church in a two-horse cutter, with a shovel in the back." The minister, who was following in his cutter, overturned, "and that's where the shovel came in handy."

A self-made man, he had acquired a small fortune by the time of his retirement. In 1927 they moved to their new University Drive house and we stayed on in the Main Street home. In March, 1940 the happy couple celebrated their Diamond wedding anniversary, and the telegram from the King and Queen, a rarity at the time, was delivered in person by the manager of CN Telegraphs. As a matter of fact, it was at their anniversary reception that I had my first experience with anything stronger than lemonade. I was sixteen at the time, not nearly as sophisticated as today's teenagers, when I managed to sneak home with two pop bottles full of wine that had been used to toast my grandparents. A friend and I knew that French and Italian youngsters were brought up on wine, so we had no qualms about drinking the entire bottle as if it had been Coca Cola. Needless to say, we got slightly blotto. Our crash course in imbibing was a little too much for our system, and not at all appreciated by our respective parents.

Our Main Street house was a two-storey structure with wood siding and a glassed-in veranda that went across the front and down one side. The concrete basement had been excavated below ground level, which was a common practise at the time. It contained a coal bin, and a cistern for collecting rainwater. The cistern was built by using two corner walls and adding two walls of concrete, approximately six inches thick and rising to within a foot of the basement ceiling. I assume that the house was built prior to the city's water system being installed, but by the time we had moved in we only used the soft rainwater in the cistern for washing hair. (Some sections on the West Side were still getting their water delivered by horse drawn wagon at fifty cents a barrel.) There was a pump for the cistern, located in the bathroom off the kitchen. In order to make it work, it had to be primed by adding glasses of tapwater while pumping the handle.

On the main floor were the kitchen, two bedrooms, a large dining room, a small living room, and an entrance hallway. Two bedrooms and storage space were located on the second floor. The kitchen had a steel and chrome coal and wood range, with a warming oven on the top of the hood, and a water reservoir on the right-hand side. The reservoir served two purposes: it helped, in a minor way, to moisten the dry hot air from the range and the coal furnace, and it was a source of hot water. The kitchen must have been added after the house was built because, instead of a basement under the kitchen, there was a three-foot earthen crawlspace. The waterpipes for the bathroom had to come from the basement and through the crawlspace, which meant that at least twice each winter the pipes froze solid when overnight temperatures hovered around 20 below and lower. The only way they could be thawed was for Grandpa to lower himself into the crawlspace, through a trapdoor located in the pantry, and heat them with a blowtorch. Another inconvenience of living through a prairie winter was the installation of storm windows in the fall, and their removal each spring. Installing and removing storm windows, on the second storey, from a rickety wooden ladder, was no easy task.

The brick chimney for the kitchen stove went up through the bathroom ceiling with an elbow through the wall to the stove. Every second or third winter we would get patches of unsightly black creosote on the bathroom ceiling, from around the elbow. We had it fixed a dozen times, but, inevitably the creosote came back. New flashings, cleaning the chimney, replacing a few bricks . . . nothing worked. It was frustrating . . . and expensive.

Behind the house, backing onto the alley, was a stable with a loft. We used it for storage and, later on, as a garage for my brother's secondhand

Penny Candy, Bobskates

Overland. Bert had a lot of fun tinkering with that car, but the fastest I ever saw it go was when three chums shoved it on the run down the lane.

The streets of Nutana run from east to west and are numbered 1 to 13. Avenues go north to south and are named. Our street was the exception to all this. Presumably the city planners in the 1920's had envisioned the street as developing into a major thoroughfare. As a result it was given the name Main, and built much wider than the average street. It was located between 9th and 10th streets, resulting in considerable confusion to deliverymen over the years. In the 1930's the street was just a dirt road with curbs, sidewalks and boulevards planted with poplar and elm. The next improvement was to gravel the road. Finally in the late '30s a boulevard was built in the middle of the street, complete with grass, bushes and curbs. But Main Street never did become a major thoroughfare. That role was taken by 8th Street, when commercial and residential development took off in that direction.

Friends of mine in the 400 block of Main Street in the early '30s included Johnny and Jimmy Schmitz (their father was chief engineer of the Big Chief Breweries); George Mackie, son of Sgt. Mackie of the City Police (later to become deputy chief); Jim Greening, member of an English family; Cecil and Bud Ross, and Jim Black. Neighbours included Miss Perry (sister of the owner of Perry's Ladies Wear on 2nd Avenue); Lois and Doreen Blackwell; and a German family by the name of Jacklic. He thought that Hitler was the best thing that ever happened to Germany, and returned with his wife and daughter to the fatherland in May, 1939. I have often wondered what happened to them.

Across the street were Don, Gorde, and Billy Munro (Dave Munro served on the Exhibition board for many years); the Buchans; the Allinghams; the Thompsons (a teacher at Nutana Collegiate); and the McPhees. At the corner of Main Street and Eastlake Avenue was the Eastlake Apartment Block, and at the other end of the street, on the corner of Victoria Avenue and Main Street, was the Ukrainian Institute, with over a hundred live-in high school students. Beside it was a three-floor walkup, called the Dorr Block, where Keith Laing lived with his widowed mother. Billy Russell and his sister, Millie, lived in the 300 block. It was really weird but on two or three occasions Millie's purse fell on the floor while we were there, and deposited the exact amount that Billy and I needed to go to the show. The damnedest thing I ever saw!

8

and Frozen Roadapples

The Braithwaite family lived near us. One of the boys, Max, would become a prominent author. And the Diefenbaker's had a house a couple of blocks behind ours. Young John was destined to lead the country in a Conservative sweep many years later.

Another friend, who lived in an old brick house across the street from the McRaes, was Gorde Terndrup. One summer's day his brother (the name escapes me) was out shooting with a .22 rifle when he was almost fatally wounded. He had leaned the rifle against a wire fence, while he climbed over the five strands of wire. The motion of the fence caused the rifle to fire, hitting him in the stomach. He was sixteen at the time, alone, and approximately three miles from the city's outskirts. He staunched the flow of blood by walking doubled over, and somehow managed to cover those three miles. All of Saskatoon was amazed by what he had accomplished, and followed the news of his gradual recovery in the *Star/Phoenix*.

Dr. Oliver, the city's coroner, lived in the 400 block on 10th Street. That was the house we all headed for when we got something in our eye, sprained an ankle, or had a badly cut hand. He would patch us up, and it didn't cost anything (socialized medicine at its best). Mrs. Margaret Munro was another person whom everyone came to rely on when a neighbourhood youngster was sick or hurt. She was a registered nurse, who willingly gave of her time to help.

From our Main Street home we could see clear out to the Exhibition Grounds, where a polar bear was kept in a small enclosure, and two or three deer in another. I guess these represented the city's zoo. But even at that, it was an exciting place to visit as a kid.

Our house was one block west of Broadway Avenue. The stores that we passed on the way to Victoria School included Mylrea's Texaco Garage, the Red Robin Cafe, Malouf's Grocery, a fur store, Barclay's Confectionery, a shoe store, a barber shop, Broadway Hardware, the Hillcrest Garage, Gibson's Photos, a shoemaker, a coffee shop, Harrington's Jewellers, and finally, at Five Corners, a drug store which later became part of the Pinder chain. On the Avenue's other side was Mulvey's Cartage and Storage, a Chinese laundry, a thread and fabric shop, the Royal Bank of Canada, the Purity Dairy, Ling's Bakery, and Victoria School. A firehall was located opposite the school. St. Joseph's Catholic Church was built at the corner of Broadway Avenue and 8th

Penny Candy, Bobskates

Street, in 1928. At the same time, St. Joseph's Elementary School was built across the Avenue in the 900 block.

There was a bicycle shop on Broadway Avenue, not much larger than a hut, at the approaches to the Broadway Bridge. It was owned by a small chap (I believe his name was Bert) who was a war veteran. The reason I remember this, is because when Mother was buying my first two-wheeler, around 1933, he told her that he had served overseas with Dad, and he gave her a reduced price on the second-hand bicycle.

The 400 block on Main Street was next to Victoria Avenue, whose commercial prominence was always overshadowed by the greater number of businesses located on Broadway. However, it had its own thriving enterprises which included, in the 1930s, Parr's Red and White Store, Clendenning's Meat Market, Tapley's Groceteria, Turner's Drug Store, Whitehead's Shoe Repair, and a candy store run by an elderly English couple. I believe their name was Clarke. The stores did a good business, helped in considerable measure by the students in residence in the Ukrainian Institute and the apartment dwellers in the Dorr Block.

By 1925, the year of our arrival, Saskatoon already had an interesting history and its population was an estimated 28,000. Back in 1890, when the Temperance Colonization Company chose the western bank of the South Saskatchewan River for its railway station, the west bank settlement became known as Saskatoon, and the east bank became Nutana. They were connected by a ferry service and a high trestle bridge. In 1901 Saskatoon was incorporated as a village, in 1903 it became a town, called Riverside, which in turn incorporated in 1905. Saskatoon soon became known as the "Hub City" because it was equal distance from the Great Lakes, Hudson Bay, and Vancouver. The city was given its name by its founder, John Lake, head of the Temperance Colony. History records that an Indian gave him a sampling of the berry they called a saskatoon, which grew in profusion along the riverbank, and he decided to name the settlement after the berry.

Saskatoon was a small, pretty city a half century ago, with attractive bridges spanning the South Saskatchewan River which meandered through the city's centre. Located in the heartland of the prairie with its unbroken horizon and vast blue sky, it was a friendly, wonderful place to grow up. From kid to adult, it was my hometown for more than twenty years. The city and the times are full of happy memories for me.

10

Summer's Free Spirits

My first recollections of Saskatoon begin around 1929, when I was six years old. I recall very vividly that the horse still played a prominent role in the city's economy. Most deliveries, including groceries, bread, milk and ice, were by horse-drawn wagon. Basements were excavated by a team pulling a digger, spurred on by the driver's lashing whip.

I spent many enjoyable hours on a summer's day watching Mr. Storey in his blacksmith shop on Broadway Avenue as he straightened ploughshares, sharpened discs, and shoed horses, his muscles bulging, his brow beaded in sweat from the white-hot flames fanned by hand-operated bellows.

And who can forget the thrill, in the heat of an August day, of following the ice man on his house deliveries, in order to get a piece of ice chipped from the large blocks.

There was a big barn — old and smelly — at the end of our block, on the corner of Main Street and Victoria Avenue. It had been there for years and, as the street developed and new houses were built, it became a real eyesore. I can remember going out on the front lawn and swatting the rump of a Clydesdale that had wandered down the sidewalk from that barn and was grazing on our grass. And then late one summer's night I was pulled out of bed in a flurry of excitement to watch out the kitchen window as the huge barn burned to the ground. It was a time of great

Penny Candy, Bobskates

rejoicing in the neighbourhood, and considerable speculation as to the identity of the local hero who started the blaze.

Tony, "the fruit man," would visit our street once a week with fresh fruit and vegetables. If you behaved yourself while he left the horse and wagon unattended, you were rewarded with a small slice of watermelon, or a few grapes. If you didn't, you would end up on the receiving end of a stream of choice Italian words that would undoubtedly not bear repeating in polite company. Tony serviced our neighbourhood for several years, trying to save enough money to bring his family out from Italy. Tragically he died a few months short of his goal.

The working life of the horse was placed on notice when the first Model T rolled off the assembly line. Various commercial enterprises in Saskatoon recognized the need to get motorized early in the changeover. The first motorized hearse was introduced in 1913 by the Saskatoon Funeral Home. That same year saw a parade of several touring cars down 21st Street. The city police soon had their first paddy wagon, and traffic patrol got their first motorcycle, complete with sidecar. Meanwhile, experiments were underway at the University of Saskatchewan to find a cheaper fuel than gasoline. In 1918, Professor R.D. McLaurin tested a McLaughlin motor car powered by gases obtained from decaying straw.

MacCosham Van Lines Ltd. had its first light delivery truck in 1920, and that same year the Saskatoon Brewing Co. was delivering its products in trucks, with dual back wheels. I remember seeing what must have been the last of the cartage trucks that had solid rubber tires and a chain-driven transmission. I believe that it was in the fleet of the Saskatoon Cartage and Storage Company.

In 1919 only the rich could afford cars, but by 1926 prices had dropped, the economy was on the upswing, and many families took out loans to purchase their first automobile. The car loans and the five-year mortgages helped to hasten the era of the Great Depression, when supply exceeded demand, forcing many businesses into bankruptcy.

I spent a good deal of time, as a kid, hanging around Mylrea's Garage on Broadway Avenue, watching the owner as he worked on cars. They were mostly Model A Fords, and the occasional Whippet, Star, Essex, Overland, Pontiac and Buick, all with wooden spokes and running boards. Sometimes Mr. Mylrea would let me hand-pump the gas to refill

and Frozen Roadapples

the cylinder after a car had taken a fill-up. And I've seen the look on Mylrea's face when, at the tail end of a long day, a car drove in with a flat tire. He would have to jack the car up, deflate the tire, remove the tire and tube, inflate the tube, place it in the basin of water so that the bubbles could tell him where the hole was, patch the tube, deflate it one more time, replace the tire and the tube onto the rim, tighten the lug nuts, pump up the tire and, finally, lower the jack. The labour was all manual, the entire procedure physically demanding. The fee was seventy-five cents.

Youngsters always looked forward to the weekend edition of the *Star-Phoenix* for their own little paper, called the *Prairie Pals*. Most kids had at least one letter published in the paper. It usually mentioned their school and grade, their hobbies and sports, and invited pen pals to write. If you had five letters published (they could be about your summer holidays, hobbies, school activities, or whatever) you were given a *Prairie Pal* pin to wear on your jacket.

It seems to me that the church played a more prominent role in our youth than appears to be the case today. This was probably due to the fact that the church of the 1930's did not have to compete with things like Little League baseball and soccer in summer, and organized hockey leagues in winter. Just about everyone I knew went to Sunday School, and joined the Cubs and Scouts or Brownies and Guides, all sponsored by the church. Girls also had a choice of joining Explorers as youngsters and Canadian Girls in Training (CGIT) in their teens. We played carpetball in the church basement, put on concerts for parents, went on Sunday School picnics, and always looked forward to the Christmas party with its entertainment and Santa and his bag full of toys.

Our Catholic friends attended church services more often than we did. I was always amazed by their early Mass. I couldn't imagine anyone going to church at seven in the morning. When I was around six or seven, I went to St. Joseph's Church with a Catholic chum on two or three occasions. I was quite taken with the pageantry of their service: the colourful robes of the priest, the burning incense, the ringing of bells, and the beautiful statuary on both sides of the pews. After that I found the protestant service to be quite boring, and told Mother that I wanted to join the Catholic church. She declined my offer.

When the Cub Pack was started around 1933 at the church where I

Penny Candy, Bobskates

attended Sunday School, Westminster Presbyterian on the corner of 12th Street and Eastlake Avenue, I was made the Senior Sixer. My sole qualification for the job was the fact that I was the only Cub with a uniform, having transferred from the pack at Grace United on 10th Street. Cubs was a lot of fun. We camped each summer at Pike Lake; participated in the annual Copper Trail; and qualified for various badges such as Woodcraft, Stamp Collector, First Aid, Gardening, Cooking and so on. We camped at Pike Lake, in tents without floors, and slept in blankets, because no one had a sleeping bag. Cooking was done over a campfire of dead branches collected from the woods. It was fun, but I think we all felt that a long weekend was the extent of our endurance at "roughing it."

One winter we went on a hike to Yorath Island, going through the Exhibition grounds and across the river. When we got there we started a bonfire and had a beanfeed. It was really quite an undertaking for youngsters; the snow was deep, making walking difficult, and it was cold. It seems to me that it was dark around four o'clock when we started for home. I recall that my bed that night felt awfully good.

Our Cub Pack held father and son beanfeeds twice a year. I always felt a little sad when they were coming up, but I usually went with a chum and his dad, and quite enjoyed myself. I will never know, of course, how much I missed not having a father. Probably the best way to put such a loss into perspective, would be for me to ask, "What did your father contribute to your life?" And my response to your reply would be, "Well, I missed all that." I can remember being teased when I was around six or seven about not having a dad (how do you spell kid? c-r-u-e-l). But I was a happy youngster by temperament, and I was not overly concerned about what was missing in my life. I am sure that the loss of a father was much more traumatic for my brother and sister, who were twelve and nine when Dad died. As I look back on my brother's life (he passed away in 1985), I suspect that the loss was deep seated and its effects long lasting.

In the '30s the Cubs and Scouts held a unique annual event called the Copper Trail. Each year on a designated Saturday Cubs and Scouts would line the curbs on Second Avenue and on 20th Street, the main business street on the West Side. The people on the street donated pennies which the youngsters laid side by side until by the end of the day a continuous trail of coins would line the curbs. Pennies are made mostly of copper, thus the name Copper Trail. That was at the time when pennies were worth something, and the collected funds were used to finance Cub and Scout activities. As the value of the penny decreased, so did the enthusiasm for organizing the event, and the last Copper Trail took place in Saskatoon around 1934.

Cub and Scout uniforms and equipment (knives, hatchets, compasses and so on) were available free of charge by collecting Libby labels. The Libby Company published a catalogue listing the various items, and the number of labels required to obtain them. It was the only way that many youngsters could get their scouting gear.

I was probably eight or nine when a burglar tried to break into our house early one morning during the summer holidays. Mother and I were alone at the time. Bert was camping at Wakaw Lake, and Pat was staying with friends in their cottage at Emma Lake. Mother came into my room around 4:30 a.m., told me not to make any noise, and that someone was trying to open our back door. She helped me to dress in the dark in a matter of seconds. We tiptoed to the kitchen. It was frightening to hear someone trying to pry the door open with some sort of tool. Mother was shaking so badly that when she went to phone the police I thought she would never finish dialling. By that time the morning light was taking over from the night, and we heard footsteps on the sidewalk that ran the length of our house. Peeking between the blind and the window, we saw a middle-aged man, wearing a suit and carrying a satchel, nonchalantly walking up the street, as though he was on an early morning stroll.

A policeman arrived about one hour later, walking. In those days, the early 1930's, when there was an emergency, the police station would telephone businesses along the policeman's route, trying to catch up with him to relay the message. But before and after closing hours it was an even slower process. In the downtown area call-boxes were installed on telephone poles, providing a direct phone service to and from the station. The constable checked the back door, and found that several holes had been punched around the lock, in an effort to displace it. The burglar apparently had used an ice pick to try and force entry. It had been a real scary morning.

Our telephone number in Saskatoon sixty years ago was 97638. What an incredible memory! I only wish I could remember where in hell I park my car.

Penny Candy, Bobskates

George Johnston was the only one I knew who had a Magic Lantern, a machine that projected slides in black and white onto a screen. Whenever he was going to have a "picture show" in his basement, he was the most popular kid in the neighbourhood. Our excitement at watching cartoon characters come to life on a screen was no less than kids had many years later, when dad bought the family's first television set.

String telephones were fun to make, but they never seemed to work very well. They were made by tying string to holes punched in the bottom of two empty tin cans. The string was at least fifteen feet long. You talked into one can, and the listener held the second one to his ear. You had to talk so loud you could be heard without the can, but you always fooled yourself into thinking that the string was actually carrying the message.

Most kids had a pair of stilts that they made from two pieces of 2-by-4 approximately six to seven feet long, with footblocks nailed some thirty inches from the end of the stilt. The higher up the footblock was attached, the trickier it was to walk. When you got reasonably accomplished at stilt walking, you would raise the blocks to four feet above the ground or more. This meant that the stilts had to be mounted from a fence or porch, unless you were willing to risk the possibility of a sprained ankle. The more adventurous would attempt to get underway by running with the stilts and jumping onto the blocks.

A summer pastime that falls under the rationale that "boys will be boys" was watching red and black ants in a fight to the death. There was a black ant colony on the boulevard in front of our house, and a red ant colony down the street. We soon learned that they didn't like each other, and we played our game by transporting some red ants, in a bottle, to the black ant colony. What the heck! We didn't have television with its violent cartoons to appeal to our baser instincts, so we had to create our own chaos.

And I can relate to the youngsters of today who are frightened by "the bomb." After all, if you're scared stiff, it doesn't really matter what caused it. Fear is fear. We didn't have "the bomb," but we had the "red hot steel dirigible," and that was enough. An older kid in the neighbourhood told me about it, when I was around four or five years of age. He told me that it came over on a real hot day in August, and when it blew up you had to be careful you weren't hit by any of the burning pieces. That did it! I was scared stiff for three long days and three longer nights until someone wisened me up. What a rotten trick! When I was eight, I played it on young Patrick Greening.

Trains were, and probably still are, fascinating to youngsters. We were very much aware of their presence because where we lived we could hear the train's whistle being blown two or three times a day as trains approached the crossing a few blocks from our house. We used to climb the 20th Street overpass and watch freight trains as they shunted boxcars back and forth in the CN yards. Every once in a while we would get caught in a belch of black smoke from an engine directly beneath us.

The university was a great place to put in time during a summer's day. We would play on the railway jigger at the back of the Engineering Building, riding it on its spur to the mainline and back again. There was always something going on at the university, even in summer. We would watch the students playing tennis, and then go over to the stadium, which was later named after their popular sports director, Joe Griffiths, and watch them practice track and field events. We often took a picnic lunch and spent the whole day at the university.

George Johnston and I used to take our lunch and hike into the country to watch the gophers and crows, listen to the song of the meadowlark, and generally commune with nature. Whenever we were near a patch of ripe berries we ate until we were full. In a good year saskatoons, chokecherries, pinchberries, and gooseberries were plentiful. They all made excellent jams and jellies, and a few made quite a decent wine. You never loaded up on chokecherries if you were far from a tap. A handful made your mouth feel like you had been sucking all day on a lemon.

One day we watched a long freight train slowly winding its way to the yards at the Exhibition. We were startled to see flames leaping out from the rear wheel of one of the cars, and we ran for what seemed like a couple of miles to tell some workmen of the impending disaster. That was the first time we heard about "hotboxes." When waste cotton, packed around the car's axel, worked its way out of the housing and came in direct contact with the revolving axle, it often caught fire from the friction. It was quite common and certainly didn't justify our heroic efforts. We were pooped by the time we got there.

17

Penny Candy, Bobskates

As we got older the trains presented a challenge to our youthful spirits. We used to cross the Grand Trunk Bridge on the ties, hoping that a train didn't unexpectedly appear on the horizon. If it did, we ran for the nearest barrel that was intended for such circumstances, and jumped in. There were approximately three such barrels that hung on both sides of the bridge, every hundred feet or so. In this case when I say "we," I mean "some of us." My fear of the water prevented me from walking on railway ties forty feet above the river. The other challenge was to grab the rung of a freight car at the foot of Main Street, as the train slowly wound its way to the CN yards, jumping off as it approached the bridge. It really wasn't any big deal, because the train was probably going about 15 mph, but we thought it was pretty daring at the time.

It's just natural for kids, especially boys, to be adventurous. When we were teenagers, one of my friends, Keith McColl, hopped the fence of the elk enclosure on the fairgrounds to get a better look at the elk. He paid the price. He was in hospital for a time, and missed a couple of months of school, but it didn't deter him from his love of animals. In recent years he has had his own outdoors program on the CTV network, and has photographed animals in their natural habitat in all four western provinces, Alaska, and countries such as Fiji and Australia.

Things happened fifty years ago that would never happen now. Floyd Williams, a neighbour and a friend of my brother, owned a large dog that had been a pet for something like twelve years. One hot summer's day we noticed that the dog was frothing at the mouth, its breathing was laboured, and it had considerable difficulty in walking. One of the neighbours was certain that it had been poisoned and called the police. A young constable arrived on the scene, took the dog into a garage, and shot it. When Floyd came home from work and was told the news, he was devastated. He called a vet to the house to examine the body, which had been placed in a potato sack. The vet diagnosed a mild stomach upset.

The neighbourhood pet was Spot, a Boston Bull that was around three years of age when it moved into the house across the alley. We soon learned that Spot would rather be swinging in circles with all four feet off the ground at the end of a potato sack than do anything else, including eat. He had an insatiable desire to be airborne. We would tire of the game, but Spot never did, and it took a great deal of willpower not to give in to his never ending appeal to play. Spot would drag the sack, growling continuously, whipping it back and forth in a frenzy, and drop it at your feet in a challenge. One day we missed our little canine tormentor, and when he didn't show up by late afternoon we knocked on the owner's door to see if he was sick. It was much worse. He was dead. He hadn't wakened from his sleep, and his owner said that his continual whirling around might have brought on a stroke. We all felt sad, and a little guilty. Maybe we shouldn't have given in so easily to his invitation to play.

I always had a dog when I was young, my children had dogs, and their youngsters have dogs. My first pet was Nellie, a beautiful black cocker spaniel. We got her when I was four, and they took her away when I was six. A family moved onto our street that had a kennel of five bulldogs, and Mother explained it to me this way: "Nellie is a girl, and those dogs won't leave her alone. So we will have to give her to a friend who lives on a farm, where she will be happy." I didn't understand what that was all about, but if it would make Nellie happy I guess that would be alright. A couple of years later I got my second dog, a bull terrier puppy, and I named him Buddy, because that is what he was. When I was lonely, or things weren't going right, I would put my arms around Buddy's neck, and tell him all about my problems. He would look at me with his big brown eyes, and I knew that he understood every word. I think that God made puppies so that little boys, no matter how bad things got, always had one loyal friend, who stuck by him when the going got rough.

Hammocks were a popular item in the '30s and many families had one. Some were quite decorative, as well as being functional, and were intended for in-house use. Hammocks were approximately seven feet long, and required two substantial supports ten to twelve feet apart. In the backyard they could be hung between two trees, or, one tree and the corner of the garage. We strung ours on the veranda, one end on the doorframe, the opposite end on the inside corner. On a rainy day it was often a race in our house to see who could have the luxury of swinging in the hammock. You soon learned, however, to handle them with a degree of caution. Not unlike a canoe, if you fooled around, over you went.

Whenever we went for a Sunday drive, it was usually to the Forestry Farm. In the late '30s, when the areas were developed, you could also choose between Yorath Island or Pike Lake. To go to the Forestry Farm we often drove through the university to look at the cows, pigs and horses, and, in the spring, to watch the lambs cavort. Then it was on to Sutherland, where you could watch the grass grow. I'm sure that if you grew up in Sutherland it was a great place, but to drive through on a Sunday was a little less than awe-inspiring. And, finally, to the farm. It was a favourite spot for family picnics, where adults could relax on the lovely lawns, and kids could play tag, or whatever. I believe there were also some horseshoe pitches, for the more ambitious. Many enjoyed walking through the flower gardens to have a look at the hollyhocks, columbines, roses, sweet peas, nasturtiums and cosmos, bordered by caragana hedges.

Another big event was the arrival each summer of the Chautauqua with its huge tent and variety acts. The Chautauqua was a tradition that probably fell victim to the Depression, as did the travelling "medicine man" shows. One of the last was set up in a vacant lot on Broadway Avenue around 1933. Advance posters on telephone poles assured a fairly good turnout for the outdoor stage show. Several amateur acts preceded the main attraction, when the Indian Chief burned the palm of his hand with a white-hot blowtorch iron, and then applied his "miracle" snakeoil remedy. "The pain is completely gone, the hand will be healed tomorrow," he exclaimed. And then proceeded to sell the snakeoil for $1.00 a bottle. The supply was quickly snapped up by the enthusiastic audience. It was a couple of days before they learned that the remedy was more malarkey than miracle.

Cairns Field was the only place in the city for holding major sports events. Each year the stands would be packed to see some visiting celebrity sports figures, like the King and His Court (a five-man softball team) play a team of local all-stars. I was always intrigued by the House of David, a hardball team whose players all had long, bushy beards.

Whether wrestling was considered a sporting event, or merely another form of entertainment, didn't matter fifty years ago, just as it doesn't matter to wrestling fans today. Matches were held from time to time in the arena, and the Hulk Hogan of the '30s was a North American Indian called Chief Thunderbird. The bad guys would gouge his face with bottle caps and split his head with folding chairs, but Chief Thunderbird remained top of the heap for a good many years. Canada's most famous wrestler in those days was "Whipper" Billy Watson. Prominent wrestlers on the various American circuits included "Strangler" Lewis, Lou Thez, who was world champion for a number of years, and a French import called "The Angel," who was far removed from angelic, and who looked a great deal like a gargoyle (with apologies to gargoyles).

When we were fifteen or sixteen, my neighbour Jim Black and I took up photography as a hobby, and we each had our own darkroom. At first we made prints from commercially produced negatives, but as we got more proficient we developed our own rolls of film. Sometimes we would go to a movie, sit through the film looking for shots that lent themselves to still photography, and then the second time around we would take photos using only the available light in the theatre. Afterwards, we would develop them to see what we got. Usually not much. But it was an interesting hobby.

I have found this exercise of recalling the things we did more than fifty years ago most interesting, and I have often been surprised at the trivial thoughts that come to mind. For instance, Jack Mackay had a "peg" tooth that he used to flip out with his tongue. It looked really weird. He had lost an upper front tooth, and the replacement had an approximate quarter-inch peg that fit into a hole in the gum. I don't really understand how it was done, but I can remember him saying that it didn't hurt to take it out whenever he wanted. In some ways we were a little envious of his "peg" tooth.

Rollerskating provided many hours of enjoyment and ruined more than one good pair of shoes. The entire skate, including the wheels, was made of steel. The skate was attached to the shoe with a buckled strap over the instep, and a clamp on the front toecap, which was tightened with a key until it pinched the shoe and bent the sole. Learning to rollerskate was quite easy because the movements are similar to those used in ice skating. Today's rollerskate is much faster with its polyurethane wheels and proper skateboot attached. I rented a pair since I retired, just to see how I could make out, and found that I was doing about five miles an hour standing still. They are fast!

Saskatoon had many interesting facets. There was quite a settlement of Metis on the outskirts of the city. A few lived in wigwams but the majority had sod houses, and made their living by cutting up small trees for firewood. Wagons full of kindling, pulled by a team of horses, were a fairly common sight in the back lanes of Nutana. On one occasion we got quite a kick out of watching one of the elderly squaws, sitting at the base of a telephone pole, wearing a man's hat and smoking a pipe, as she waited for her mate to unload the wagon.

Within months of Tony the fruit man passing away, a Chinese fruit and vegetable peddlar by the name of Eng had taken over the route. Things were different by now, and the produce arrived at our door in a truck. The horse and wagon were slowly but surely disappearing from the streets of Saskatoon. Every Christmas Eng would give his regular customers pieces of ginger or the bulb of a Chinese lily. Mother used to place the bulb in a dish, on a bed of marbles or stones, and water it daily until it bloomed.

A common sight on 2nd Avenue in the summer was another Tony, the "popcorn man," with his two-wheeled cart. It was difficult to walk by the wagon, with its aroma of popping corn, and not buy a bag. Someone once told me that Tony owned a lovely home, and put his two sons through university from the proceeds of his little two-wheeled cart.

During the summer the Salvation Army held curbside services at various locations downtown, on the West Side, and in Nutana. Youngsters couldn't quite figure out what they were all about, and referred to them as the "Sally Ann drumbeaters" (there was always a large bass drum in their small band). It was some years later that we came to respect who they were, and what they did.

We used to go on wiener roasts at night with the Schmitz family, usually on the riverbank opposite the sanatorium. After we had eaten our fill of wieners and roasted all of the marshmallows, we would have a sing-along, sometimes accompanied by an accordion. There were six girls in the Schmitz family and they were all musical. I don't know that people do that any more, but it was really fun. Maybe outdoor barbecues have done away with that summertime custom. Usually there was a full moon shining in a cloudless night, stars were twinkling brightly across the broad prairie sky, and the glowing embers from the fire cast light and shadows on our faces as we sang songs that fit our mood. "Goodnight, sweetheart, till we meet tomorrow; goodnight, sweetheart, sleep will banish sorrow."

and Frozen Roadapples

"Red sails in the sunset, way out on the sea . . ." And then, "I'm forever blowing bubbles, pretty bubbles in the air . . ." "We were sailing along on moonlight bay . . ." Finally a couple of songs from the war years, "It's a long way to Tipperary, it's a long way to go," and the one we always saved for last, "There's a long, long trail awinding into the land of my dreams . . ." It was really neat.

Some nights, not very often, there would be a display of northern lights that was better than any fireworks display I've seen to this day. The purple, green and yellow lights would flicker and dance in the heavens for an hour or more. A fantastic sight that may well be reserved for prairie folk, because I have never seen their like on the West Coast. Another phenomenon that Nother Nature bestowed on the Prairies were those magnificent thunder and lightning storms. Fork, sheet and bolt lightning would flash across the skies, followed by claps of thunder that rocked our house to its foundation.

One rainy afternoon during the summer holidays Don Thomson and I bought a box of marshmallows from the Red Robin. I believe they were called "Moonlight Mallows," and there were twenty-four to the box. We sat in the back of his dad's car and roasted them on a table fork with a box of wooden matches. We ate the whole damn box! And our parents wondered why we didn't feel like eating supper. Mom wanted to give me a tablespoon of cascara and send me to bed! (In our house the two remedies for any illness were either cascara or cod liver oil.)

Pioneers used to say that Saskatoon had five seasons: black fly, mosquito, house-fly, horse-fly . . . and winter. I can recall efforts to help control two of these seasons, the mosquito and the house-fly. Each spring the Chamber of Commerce used to sponsor a mosquito control truck which had the job of locating all water breeding sources (sloughs, swamps, etc.) within a five-mile radius of the city, and spraying the surfaces with oil. The oil killed the mosquitos' pupae, and proved to be reasonably successful in eliminating the pest. A good friend and neighbour, Gorde Munro, was killed one year when his mosquito control truck hit a big pothole on a country road, causing the huge oil tank to break loose, pinning him in the cab. He was eighteen.

The house-fly was always a problem but it was controlled to some extent by means of sticky paper hung from the doors, windows and ceilings. Flies were attracted by the smell, stuck to the paper, and expired within minutes. Strips of paper, dotted with dozens of flies, were a common sight in houses, stores and restaurants in the '30s. Uncle Dave had a friend who was down on his luck and it's quite possible that the house-fly saved him from starving. You see, before going into a cafe for a meal, he would pick up a dead fly. When his meal was almost finished, he placed the fly on the remaining food and then raised hob with the cook. He always got the meal for nothing.

The dust storms in those days were quite awesome. I do not believe there has been anything quite like them since, in terms of numbers and density. They would be similar to the heavy fogs that I have experienced on the west coast. Farmers could not afford to buy seed, and the neglected topsoil soon powdered in the unrelenting heat. You certainly didn't go outside at the storm's peak, unless absolutely necessary. Visibility was limited to half a city block. Mother used to dust the house in an attempt to keep it clean, and within a couple of hours, I could write my name on our round oak dining room table. I guess that's where the term "Dirty Thirties" came from. Grandpa used to call a dust storm "a black blizzard."

Another freak of nature that was most unpleasant were the hordes of grasshoppers that invaded the city. Backyard vegetable gardens would be stripped within two or three days, and houses were stained with the brown liquid they expectorated, which kids likened to tobacco juice. The American government sent a team of photographers across the farm states to record the plight of the farmer, so that the general public would have a better understanding of conditions caused by the drought. They were paid $30 per week and two cents per mile for their cars.

One summer a team of daredevil drivers, I think they were called the "Hell Drivers," brought their cars to the airport. A huge crowd went out to watch the stunt drivers, and whenever they made a fast spin or turn, the dust clouds were unbelievable. Bush pilots also performed one year, and I remember seeing a Ford Trimotor on display. You could go for a ride in a two-seater open cockpit, for one cent per pound. If you had the nerve!

Hot summer days were ideal for games like *Aunty-Over* (a ball would be thrown over the roof of a house, with teams on either side); *Red-Light* (where colours were yelled out, depending how close you were getting to the one in hiding. "Red" for real close, "green" for far away, "amber" for fairly close, and so on); *Hide 'N' Seek*; *Mother, Mother — May I?*; *Can-Can* (patterned after cricket); *I-Spy*; *Simon-Says*; and, of course, hopscotch, marbles, dibs and skipping.

For the more adventurous there was *Knock Down Ginger*, where you knocked on someone's front door and then ran for your life. *One O'Cat* was a game played with a bat and ball and a minimum of four to five players (pitcher, catcher, 1st baseman, and one or two fielders). The batter had to connect with the ball before strike three was called on him, and then run and tag 1st base, and get home before being tagged out. In this game there wasn't any "base on balls" given. When you were out, you went into the field, and each player moved up one position. That way everybody got a chance at bat. When there were enough bodies for a game of softball, two captains would alternately choose players for his team, until everyone was picked. The team to be first "at bat" was decided by tossing the bat to one of the captains, who caught it with a one-handed grip. The other captain placed his hand around the bat, on top of the first captain's hand, and they alternated, hand over hand, until one hand went over the top of the handle. That particular captain was declared the loser, and the other team got to bat first.

Another game that was a lot of fun was *Ball-Tag*, played with a rubber ball and with as few as two kids or as many as a couple of dozen. The idea was to hit someone with the ball and then they were "it."

It's a little surprising to think that Yo-Yo's were as popular sixty years ago as they are today. Even then we had city, provincial, and national tournaments sponsored by the manufacturer. The young champions (anywhere from fourteen to nineteen years of age) would tour Canada giving demonstrations of extremely difficult tricks. We also had *Bat-a-Ball*, a small rubber ball attached to a wooden paddle by a six-foot rubber band. It was great for hand-eye coordination.

Fishing in the river was always a thrill, but first you had to catch a supply of grasshoppers to use as bait, or dig a can of garden worms. Grasshoppers were usually plentiful, but sometimes finding enough worms was difficult.

Neighbours of ours for as long as we lived in Saskatoon were the Schmitz family. The father was the head engineer at the Big Chief

Penny Candy, Bobskates

Breweries for many years. One summer's morning he took his two sons, Johnny and Jimmy, and myself, fishing at the foot of the brewery before the start of his eight o'clock shift. We got up at about six a.m., which at eight years of age, was a thrill in itself. Mr. Schmitz had proper fishing tackle and we had grocery string that had been toughened with tar. We baited our hooks with grasshoppers and threw the line, weighted with a stone, out into the river. Before too long, with much whooping and hollering, I pulled in a goldeye which probably weighed under one pound, but which I was sure was at least two feet long. Shortly afterwards, Mr. Schmitz got his fish hook caught through his thumb, so that you could see the point under his thumbnail. We just about had a bird but he, very calmly, clipped the line, leaving the hook embedded in his thumb, went up to the brewery, froze his thumb, shoved the barbed point through the nail, clipped off the point, and pulled the hook back through the thumb. Then he went to work. That was some exciting morning.

Johnny, Jimmy, and I delivered flyers one summer for a grocery store on Broadway Avenue. Johnny was paid 10 cents because he was the supervisor, and we received a nickel each. I recall that on extremely hot days a number of flyers were shoved down storm drains just to get rid of them.

A bat and ball game, called "*500*," rivaled *One-O'Cat* in popularity because it could be played by only three players if no more were on hand. The person at bat hit the ball to the fielders, and if it was caught in the air that person got 100 points. If it was a grounder, the fielder stopping the ball rolled it from where he was to the bat, that had been placed on the ground. If he hit the bat he got 50 points. The first person to get 500 points got a turn at bat.

A popular game in our teen years was hardball, but it called for a large lot (probably a school yard) and a minimum of fourteen players, preferably eighteen for two complete teams. I was surprised to learn in later years that baseball originally started with nine balls and three strikes, but in 1888 it became the current four and three.

Buck-Buck was, without a doubt, the most physical of all the games we played in our early teens. There were two teams, each with a minimum of five a side. One team lined up in a leap-frog stance, with interlocking arms around the waist, and the head of the line wrapped his arms around

and Frozen Roadapples

a tree or telephone pole, for support. The second team took turns, one at a time, running and jumping onto the backs of the first, trying to get one of them to break their hold. When someone did cave in, the teams changed places. I learned the hard way, that when someone twenty or thirty pounds heavier than you lands on your back after a running jump, it's tough not to lose your grip.

A game that we played all through our school years, which only needed two players, was called *Scissors-Paper-Rock*. At the count of three the players formed their right hand into a rock (a fist), paper (the flat hand) or scissors (two fingers). The rules stated that paper covered rock, scissors cut paper, and rock broke scissors. The winner held his opponent's arm and hit his wrist as hard as he could with his index and third finger. We found that it stung more if you first moistened your two fingers. Come to think of it, we must have been masochists. If you followed this game with *Buck-Buck* you could wind up with a few aches and pains.

As a matter of fact in our teen years we had a couple of games that proved beyond a shadow of a doubt that the male of the species has a deeply ingrained streak of stupidity and meanness that surfaces in what we called fun. A couple of games that I can recall seemed to have the intent of permanently disabling participants. In the first, you were told to stand as limp as you could possibly get without falling over. Your friend held one of your hands in both of his, all the while imploring you to relax. . .a difficult thing to do, given the sense of impending doom which you knew only to well was coming. Suddenly without warning he would jump three feet into the air, and, as he dropped to his knees, he whipped your arm with all the strength he could muster. This had the not surprising effect of sending an incredibly sharp pain through your shoulder, up your neck, into your brain, and out of your head in a blinding, white light. It was really neat. My gawd, but we were stupid! The other game was played in the classroom in the teacher's absence. In the usual classroom setup boys sat in rows on one side of the room, girls on the other. This was not by the teacher's arrangement, but simply the natural segregation of the sexes at that stage of their teens. This game was really quite simple. The boy sitting behind you hit you on the shoulder with his fist as hard as he possibly could, while you sat perfectly still. You

27

then hit the fellow in front of you, and so on. I had the great misfortune of sitting between two of the biggest hunks in the class. I can recall being hit so hard I vibrated like Woody Woodpecker does when he flies into a brick wall. I would sit there for a couple of minutes with double vision. Then, when I felt that I could move without danger of passing out, I would hit the chap in front of me. My blow, I suspect, was somewhat akin to being hit with a marshmallow at some distance! What wonderfully innocent games we played! The kind of games you can never forget! Fifty years later you have the bursitis to remind you!

When you were around twelve or thirteen and if you had a chum who owned a .22 rifle, it was always fun to hike into the country and shoot gophers or crows. There wasn't any bounty on gophers, but you could get two cents for each pair of crow's feet you brought back, and one cent for each crow and magpie egg. The first couple of times I used a .22 rifle, I went with my friend, Erwin Schellenberg, and his dad. (Mr. Schellenberg and his brothers owned and operated the OK Economy chain of grocery stores.) We fired Whiz Bang .22 shorts, because it was the cheapest ammunition available. When I was considered reliable enough to go on my own with friends, we used to take bottles and tin cans with us into the country for target practice. That didn't prove too popular with the farmers whose land we happened to be on at the time. That was especially true when one of us missed the target one time and hit a cow. The veterinary charges were $15.00.

Another popular pastime was to roll hoops, available from empty kegs or barrels, with a crossed stick made from lathing. The more dextrous made arrow guns from a piece of tongue-in-groove wood, with arrows carved from shingles, fired by a rubber band cut from a bike's inner tube.

Our arsenal also included a pea shooter, a BB gun, and a rubber-band gun. The pea shooter actually was more effective with tapioca, and we soon learned that a 16-inch barrel was better than a 6-inch barrel, because the increased length added to the velocity and accuracy. BB guns were quite a luxury and very few kids owned one. My chum was loading his one day, with the rifle butt on the ground and the thumb of his left hand gripping the top of the barrel. When he pulled the lever the gun went off and a BB, that he didn't know was in the gun, hit his thumb. He never did that again. Everybody owned a rubber-band gun. The small ones fired the rubber-bands used in offices, the larger ones used bands cut from bicycle tubes. They smarted when they hit. The interesting thing, as I look back, was that nearly all of the playthings we used as kids were handmade. Today's youngsters have been pretty much deprived of that pleasure.

We used to play bike polo on the grounds of Nutana Collegiate. The mallets were made from broomsticks, and large spools from a shoemaker's shop. Two teams would chase a tennis ball from goal to goal, and it took a bit of doing before you learned not to put the mallet through the spokes of your front wheel on the follow-through from a hefty swing.

We grew up on wheels. As youngsters we had tricycles. Around age six or seven (or whenever your parents could afford it) you got your first two-wheeler. I rode my trike on two wheels for blocks at a time until my grownup bike came along. In those days it was trikes, then bikes, nothing fancy. . .that was it. A day didn't go by, weather permitting, that we didn't spend at least an hour biking. And we got pretty clever at what we could do. We would ride three to a bike. . .one friend sat on the handlebars and another on the seat, while you pedalled standing up. Or we would try what we had see them do in the circus. Five on a bike at one time. . .the last two on either side of the back wheel with one foot each on the axle, and holding hands to keep from falling. We did a lot of "no hands" riding, but probably the neatest and most difficult trick of all was to ride your bike backwards, sitting on the handlebars. You soon learned to turn opposite to the direction you were about to fall, and it was amazing how proficient we became. Experience, however, was a tough teacher. I was in the house one day when I heard screaming like all hell had broken loose. When I dashed outside, I found that the source of the anguish was my friend Jimmy. He had been riding on the handlebars of his brother's bike, his bare feet dangling in front, when one had become entangled in the spokes. The result was a badly sprained ankle.

If one of your friends was lucky enough to come up with a used truck tire you were in for a real hair-raising ride. You curled up inside the tire and had someone push you down the street. It was even better (or worse, depending on your point of view) if you could find a hill with a gentle slope and, preferably, no trees at the bottom.

Penny Candy, Bobskates

Prior to the landscaping of the riverbanks the trees grew in great profusion and the "jungle" they created was a popular playground for youngsters. You could hike among them, climb up them, and make a variety of playthings out of their branches and bark. I think that everybody had at least one slingshot (not always with their parents' permission). This called for just the right-sized branch with the proper fork in it. And most tried their hand at making a whistle out of a willow branch. You needed a piece four or five inches long and no bigger than one-half inch in diameter. The bark was loosened by tapping it with a stick until it slid off in one piece. The tricky part was in the amount of wood you scraped off, for the passage of air, and in the fashioning of the mouthpiece. With any luck you came up with a whistle that changed notes as you slid the loose bark up and down. Making a "speargrass flute" was much easier. You stuck a broad blade of grass between your thumbs and blew. It took a bit of doing to get it right. Finally there was the musical comb. A piece of tissue paper was folded over the comb's teeth and by humming on the paper you got the same sound as a kazoo. And I hate to think of the number of birch trees we spoiled in seeing who could get the largest single piece of bark out of the trunk.

In the spring when the cotton drifted down from the poplar trees that lined many of the boulevards in Nutana, it would accumulate against the curb like a miniature snowdrift. When you lit one end of it you could watch it burn, like a fireworks sparkler, for the entire block. You had to make sure that there weren't any cars parked at the curb (more than one had its gas tank ignited by the flames).

Summer activities usually included hiking, tennis, fishing, biking and swimming. Older kids would bike to Yorath Island, or Pike Lake, for a day's swimming. The city's only public pool was located on the West Side. It was a long walk from Nutana, but a nickel and a couple of transfers would get you there on the streetcar, or trolley, as they were known. Anyone who was ever a passenger on one that went over a railway bomb that some youngster had pilfered from the CN roundhouse will never forget the experience. The bombs were used as signals to warn locomotive engineers, and the noise scared you out of ten years' growth.

Here comes another childhood confession. We raided gardens! Why? Because it was dark, because there was nothing else to do, and because you had decided that a big, fresh carrot would taste just great. What I am not too happy about, as I look back, is that often we would grab handsful of six or more lovely carrots, when we only needed one each. The others would be left in the back lane, probably to rot. We also raided a few apple trees, but a bad dose of the green apple "quick-step" discouraged any further forays.

Kites were not overly popular in the '30s, and they certainly weren't as sophisticated as they are today, but a boy usually tried his hand at making at least one. Two strips of wood from an apple box were whittled down to just the right width, and tied together with grocery string to form the cross-shaped frame. Brown wrapping paper was then applied to both sides of the frame, and the edges were held fast with mucilage. The final step in the process of kite making was to add the tail which consisted of a long piece of string through which small pieces of newspaper were looped, giving the appearance of approximately twelve paper bows on a fifteen-foot tail. The kite was now ready for flight. The lack of success in making a decent kite was probably the reason why kite flying did not enjoy too much popularity. The brown wrapping paper and wooden frame usually made the end product too heavy to be aerodynamic. Once it was airborne (if at all), and provided the breeze was strong enough, the kite could be a thing of beauty. But more often than not, it became torn from numerous unsuccessful attempts to get it to fly, and was discarded in favour of something that was more fun and less frustrating.

A jack-knife was a boy's most prized possession. He used it to whittle sticks, to carve arrows from shingles for arrow guns, and to make willow whistles. But mostly he used it for a game called *Knives*. The game was played by touching all ten fingers, one at a time, with the point of the big blade, and then flipping the knife into the boulevard (bare ground was usually too hard). The knife had to stick so that you could get at least two fingers between the blade and the ground. When the knife failed to stick properly it was the next person's turn, and when the ten fingers were completed you proceeded to the wrist, the elbow, the shoulder and finally, the chin. The game was real popular and helped pass a lot of time.

One thing that wasn't fun about summer holidays was the fear that went around, usually in August, of the dreaded INFANTILE PARALYSIS. Even the name was scary. As soon as the radio or

Penny Candy, Bobskates

newspapers announced the arrival of the first case for that summer, your parents were always checking to make sure that you didn't have a headache or a sore throat. The threat of polio scared everyone, until Dr. Salk invented his marvellous vaccine in the 1950's.

Coca Cola held a real popular promotion in our district one summer in the mid-'30s. During a three week period they gave away six-packs of Coca Cola, one per household per week. The truck would park in the middle of the block and you helped yourself. The driver told us to take only one six-pack per family, and I never knew anyone who broke his trust. Maybe that was another sign of the times. Though the Depression made everyone hard up, people continued to hold the same ideals of honesty and sharing that had typified the days of the pioneers.

In the early '30s the largest and most popular nursery, with a huge assortment of flowers and vegetables, was the Chinese nursery near the exhibition grounds. Grandpa would go there every spring for bedding plants, and once a week in the summer, usually on our Sunday drive, we would buy our fresh vegetables. As a youngster I was intrigued by two or three elderly gentlemen with white flowing beards sitting in what was the living quarters of the nursery smoking long-stemmed pipes without any discernible movement. If it wasn't for the smoke that curled upwards from their mouths, you would have thought they were wax figures. I remember how fascinated I was one summer, delivering handbills on 1st Street, when I came upon a Chinese mother and daughter hobbling around on tiny feet bound in leather. I could hardly wait to get home and tell Mother what I had seen. She explained that for many years the Chinese did not think it was ladylike to have large feet, so they started the custom of binding the feet of little girls, practically from infancy. This unusual, and extremely painful custom, was done away with several years ago, and is only practised to this day in very remote regions of China.

We took up five-pin bowling in our pre-teens, and spent many happy hours in a basement bowling alley located downtown. For the life of me I cannot recall either the name or location of the alley. We paid 10 cents a game, and I think that I got as much fun out of watching the pin boys as I did out of bowling. I always thought that their very lives were in danger. They sat, with their feet up, on a four-foot railing that separated the lanes, and were responsible for setting pins in the lanes on either side of

and Frozen Roadapples

their railing. I used to watch in awe as some husky bowler threw a ball as if it were fired from a cannon, and the pins would fly in every direction, some of them just missing the pin boy. Occasionally their luck ran out, and they would be hit. The other hazard they faced came from the novice bowler, who would pick up his ball from the return and, without properly looking, would lob the ball while the pin boy was still setting the pins. I did that one time, and I was horrified as I watched my ball roll down the alley. The lad had just set the last pin in place, when the ball hit it head-on. Both the ball and the pin missed him by inches and, although I couldn't hear what he was yelling at me over the din of twenty busy alleys, I got the message. Pin boys were a special breed, whose part-time livelihood gradually lost out to automation.

A few years later, when I turned sixteen, I got my driver's licence, and the thrill then for a teenager was no less than it is today. But it was a lot easier. We didn't have to write any exam or take a driver's road test. You merely went down to city hall, showed proof of age, confirmed that someone had shown you how to drive, and the licence was yours.

My grandfather would usually let me have his 1928 Pontiac for a couple of hours on the weekend, and I would take my friends for a drive. Within my first six months of being licensed, I had the misfortune of hitting a city bus on 8th Street near the Lutheran College, and was charged with driving on the wrong side of the road. The summons had to be delivered to me in person. The police made several trips to our house before finding me at home. Mother was having a fit because she was sure that the neighbours would think I had suddenly become No. 1 on the police "most wanted" list. The summons read, "The City of Saskatoon versus Robert H. Thompson" and I felt completely outnumbered.

I was scared stiff as I sat in the courtroom, and when the court clerk yelled, "Oyey, oyey, oyey," to announce the magistrate's entrance, I jumped about ten feet. No one had warned me about this court formality, and I was sure someone had been noticed making a break for freedom. I got off with a $10 fine.

A trip by car to most places in Saskatchewan fifty or sixty years ago was an adventure in itself that could, at times, be frightening. The highways were mostly gravelled, but those that weren't were clay, and that could be a problem. If the weather was decent the trip could be very

Penny Candy, Bobskates

pleasant. It was when it rained that the trouble began. The clay turned to gumbo, and the trick was to drive in first gear at no more than ten to twelve miles per hour. If you were lucky you would make it, otherwise you slipped and slithered until you either stalled the engine or spun into the ditch. We made a couple of trips to Marshall, near Lloydminster, around 1931, to check on the operation of my grandfather's farm which was being run on a lease basis. The one time that it rained on a good part of our trip we wondered if we would ever get there. One of the river crossings near North Battleford was by means of a two-car ferry, pulled by a team of horses on the opposite bank. The ferry was at the bottom of a long hill, on both sides of the crossing, and the roads were like thick grease. The ferry operator had a good thing going, because he not only got paid for the river passage, he would pull you out of the ditch with his team of horses for a nominal $10.

In Marshall the hotel room Mother and I stayed in had a coiled rope, to be used in case of a fire, a wash basin, and a commode. One end of the rope was bolted to the floor and the other end was to be thrown out of the window. I guess that while you were climbing down the rope you kept hoping that the fire didn't reach the rope before you reached the ground.

The Burma Shave company had its famous advertising campaign in full swing in the '30s, and their messages could be seen on most highways throughout North America. There were usually five signs in each message, spaced approximately thirty yards apart, so that you could read the entire message as you sped down the highway. The one I remember read: His Tenor Voice . . . She Thought Divine . . . Till Whiskers Scratched . . . Sweet Adelaine . . . Burma Shave. It was an extremely popular promotion and people exchanged the various messages they had collected in their travels.

Even a Sunday outing to Watrous was not without its perils. On one trip I recall we packed a picnic lunch, left early in the morning and drove into a rainstorm halfway there. We came across a car on its side in the ditch, with the mother and two children perched on the motor in order to keep out of the mud. She told us that no one had been injured and that her husband had gone looking for a farmer with a team of horses.

Main Street was often a sea of mud when it rained, and after it had dried, the ruts created by cars made it extremely difficult to navigate, particularly on a bike. When I delivered groceries for Parr's Red & White Store, I would get in trouble when customers phoned in to complain about cracked eggs. The eggs were crated in fibreboard cartons and it was next to impossible not to crack one or two, as you made your delivery crossing from one rut to the other.

When we got into our teens, tennis and golf became our favourite summer sports. I joined the Main Street Tennis Club (my sister was the club secretary), and eventually became quite a good player. I sometimes played with my Catholic friends on the courts next to St. Joseph's church on Broadway Avenue. Our first attempts at golf took place on the Exhibition course and, on occasion, on the one near the sanatorium with the sand greens. When you finished putting you used a long-handled mop to smooth out the rut created by your ball. Though primitive by today's standards, those sand greens did have one distinct advantage. If you wanted to make sure your putt would drop, you merely made a rut with your club handle from the ball to the cup. Our putting game was never better! Bob Roberts and I inveigled his dad to come with us one day. I wanted help in correcting a horrible slice. When he saw me tee off on the first hole, he was more than a little startled. "How can I help you correct your slice if you're going to hold the club cross-handed?" I changed my grip. It was the way I had always played softball and *One-O'Cat*.

In my high school years I spent a good deal of time with the Roberts in their 7th Street home. Older daughter Pat was in training as a nurse and often had student nurses over for a home-cooked meal. Bob and I stayed close to home when they were visiting. Younger sister Shirley was a great little pianist, and I used to get her to play "Bumbleboogie" for me. Sometimes I would help Mrs. Roberts shine her hardwood floors by shoving a heavy floor polisher across them, with a piece of flannel placed under the iron block. I think it weighed something like fifteen pounds. It was a good workout.

When teenagers and young adults wanted a place to go for dancing and general hi-jinks in Saskatoon in the '30s, it was the Cave Ballroom located in the basement of the Avenue Building on 3rd Avenue and, I believe, 21st Street. The name was most appropriate because you went down a long flight of stairs and entered a huge room with a sackcloth ceiling that gave the appearance of a cave. Everyone was amused by the

Penny Candy, Bobskates

life-size caveman and woman painted on the restroom doors. I worked in the cloakroom one winter evening, when I was around sixteen or seventeen. It was all that either the management or I could take. There must have been three hundred patrons, all of them leaving at the same time, each with a coat, a hat, a scarf, and a pair of galoshes. Several went home that night in clothes they had never seen in their lives.

One year we heard that Grey Owl, the naturalist and famous Indian author, was living in a house on Lansdowne Avenue. We went to his home and caught a glimpse of him in his living room. Years later it was revealed that Grey Owl was, in fact, an Englishman married to an Indian. He had fooled a good many for a number of years.

One summer, probably around 1934-35, I helped, but mostly watched, as John and Jim Schmitz and their neighbour Jim Greening, insulated the Schmitz's two-storey frame home. After building a scaffolding, they proceeded to remove the facing boards, located under the eaves, to expose the wall joists. They then poured sack after sack of wood shavings between the joists, and packed the chips by periodically dropping a weight into the space, on the end of a rope. Wood shavings were all that was available for insulating, in those days, but they must have posed a terrible fire hazard. Prior to pouring in the last sack, we all signed our names on a piece of cardboard, with the date, and dropped it between the joists. The house was demolished in the 1980s to make room for an apartment building, and I've often wondered if the workmen ever came across our piece of cardboard.

In 1935 an event of national importance took place in Saskatoon with the opening of the Bessborough Hotel by the Governor General, the Earl of Bessborough. It was a year or two later that his successor, Lord Tweedsmuir, held a public reception in the hotel. A friend and I waited in the receiving line in great anticipation, and finally, when my turn came, an aide announced in a loud voice, "Master Robert Thompson." I then proceeded up the specially built platform to meet the Governor General and his party. I was impressed at the time at how frail he and his son looked.

I got to know the manager's son and we endeared ourselves to the hotel staff by racing through the downstairs corridors in small carts used for transporting linen. I was quite adept at manoeuvring small vehicles,

and Frozen Roadapples

having earned my wings in soap-boxes built on four rollerskates and racing down the Short Hill by the collegiate. The beauty of rollerskates was that the chassis was so close to the pavement it was virtually impossible to turn the soap-box over. An experience I had on my bicycle was not nearly as foolproof. A chum and I had agreed to get at opposite sides of the school campus and race at full speed towards each other. At the last minute he was to turn left and I would turn right, thereby having the thrill of a narrow escape. It didn't work out that way, due to the fact that when we faced each other his left and my right were on the same side. That learning experience cost us two front wheels, bruises and lacerations.

In 1936 Mother and I took the CN to Vancouver to visit my aunt and uncle. That was some holiday. Going through the mountains, trying to undress in my upper berth, eating meals in the dining car as the scenery sped by our window, those were all first-time experiences for me. The best part was to sit in the open observation car and watch the ribbons of steel unfold as the train travelled at thirty, forty, and sometimes fifty miles per hour. The conductor always had to clear the car as the train approached a tunnel entrance, and I wondered at the time if he ever had a bad day and was a minute or so too late. The only problem with the open car was that you got soot from the coal burning engine in your hair, on your clothes, and unfortunately, sometimes in your eyes. When the train pulled into Banff, a young friend and I got off and went to the station's refreshment booth to buy ice cream cones. Our curiosity must have got the better of us, and as we walked around the station, eating our cones, we somehow missed the conductor's "All Aboard." The next thing we knew we saw our train slowly proceeding up the track. We ran as fast as we could, caught up to the observation car, and pulled ourselves in by climbing up the wrought iron railing. It was a close call.

The lad, whom I had met on the train, startled me that night when we were playing cards on the little table that shoved into a slot under the window at your seat. He told me to look under the table. He had rolled his pantleg up, revealing an artificial leg. I was really surprised because he hadn't shown any signs of a limp when he walked, nor did he appear to have any difficulty in running for the train. Apparently he had lost the leg in an accident when he was six and had adjusted remarkably well to the

Penny Candy, Bobskates

handicap.

The Royal Visit on June 3, 1939, by King George VI and Queen Elizabeth, had to be the biggest celebration the city had ever held. It was a terribly exciting time for young and old alike. Children were let out of school to congregate at various points throughout the tour route, to stand for hours hoping to catch a glimpse of the royal party. School students throughout the province took part in organized activities. In Saskatoon a human flag composed of seven hundred students, each bearing the colour red, white, or blue, formed a Union Jack in front of the Massey Harris building, in honour of Their Majesties' arrival at the CN station.

Because we thought it would be a good vantage point, and probably less crowded than most, Mother and I went to my grandparents' house on University Drive to see the King and Queen on their way to visit the university. We stood on the boulevard for a couple of hours in the hot sun. But when the procession finally arrived, I missed seeing the royal couple as I peered intently into the viewfinder of my Brownie camera, hoping to come up with an historic photograph. When the film was developed, I had a rather blurred picture of the rear-end of their open touring car! I found out where and when the royal train would be leaving, and I placed pennies on the track so that they could be flattened as the train left the city. I still have one.

As I look back over all the things we did during the summer, there isn't any question that we had an awful lot of fun as youngsters growing up in the 1930's. I think a major reason was the fact that we were allowed to be "just kids." No uniforms, no equipment, no coaches, no parents yelling at us from the stands. Just a couple of kids, or a couple of dozen kids, who got together for a game of sandlot ball, or *Hide-and-Seek*, or whatever. Free spirits, doing their own thing.

Exhibition Week

I'm quite sure that if you were to ask any number of old-timers who grew up in Saskatoon during the '30s, what their favourite time of the year was, the great majority of them would say, "Exhibition Week." The remainder probably were among the fortunate few whose parents were well enough off that they could spend their vacation at their cottage at one of the four popular summer resorts, lakes Waskesieu, Wakaw, Emma or Watrous.

Exhibition week rivalled Christmas for the excitement it created in kids' minds. As soon as the dates were announced by the board of the Industrial and Agricultural Exhibition, the excitement began to grow, and it reached fever pitch by parade day.

The fair was nearly always held during the second or third week of August. The timing was just right because summer holidays were becoming a bore by then, and after the fair was over thoughts of school occupied your mind for the next couple of weeks — new teachers, new studies, new friends. Parents always said that when Exhibition week was done, summer was over, and winter not far behind.

The Traveller's Day Parade, held on the Friday before the Exhibition began, was always a fun day. It was sponsored by the United Commercial Travellers, many of whom marched in the parade wearing white slacks, blazers and straw hats called "boaters." You would try to

Penny Candy, Bobskates

get down to the parade route at least one-half hour before it began, to stake your claim on a decent vantage point. Kids were never allowed to drink anything after breakfast that morning (public restrooms were few and far between).

The parade usually led off with units from HMCS Unicorn, followed by a contingent from the Saskatoon Light Infantry. Then, for the next two hours or more, you gaped in wonderment at the floats, the pretty costumes, the drill teams, the horses, the fire engines, the decorated cars and bicycles, and laughed at the silly antics of the clowns. The highlight of the whole parade, for me, was the appearance of the circus calliope, playing its own special kind of steam whistle music, pulled by a team of prancing horses with brass and leather trappings. It was sure one exciting day. After standing for the better part of three hours, you went home to rest up for the fair that began on the Monday morning.

The Royal American "Show Train" arrived in the city on Sunday evening, having travelled all day from its previous engagement. Hundreds of spectators would go out to watch the long train unload. Elephants pulled huge wagons down from the flatcars on the railway siding, working in the light of flares. The night air was punctuated with shouts from the roustabouts: "Watch out for the elephants!" . . . "Get that kid away from the elephants!" . . . as three to four hundred sightseers crowded the siding. Each wagon, full of rides and concessions, was pulled to the midway site some two city blocks from the tracks. It was a fun evening. Unloading was usually finished sometime between 11 p.m. and midnight, and then you drifted onto the fairgrounds to watch the roustabouts set up the midway with its rides, sideshows, gambling booths, souvenir stands, and eating concessions. By early morning the bald prairies had been changed into a youngster's wonderland.

The Royal American Shows dominated the fairground and more or less shoved the industrial and agricultural aspects of the Exhibition into the background. Prize winning horses, cattle, sheep and pigs were no match for the excitement generated by the midway.

When you were real young, you had to go to the fair with your parents, which probably meant that you only went the one day. However, when you got to be ten or eleven you were allowed to go with a friend or two, and that was really great because you would go every day. We would

and Frozen Roadapples

sneak over the fence whenever we could get away with it, but as the number of "sneakers-in" increased so did the security, and they soon began patrolling the fence on horseback. That made it difficult, but not impossible. Our efforts to outwit the admission gate were worthwhile because, although seventy-five cents would go a long way on the midway, it would go much further if you didn't pay the twenty-five cent admission. The "Herman Gates" at the foot of Herman Avenue were one of two entrances. They had been opened in the middle 1920's, and were built in honour of a former owner or publisher of the *Star-Phoenix*.

The midway had a special noise that was made up of people shouting on the various rides, combined with the calliope-type music of the merry-go-round, and the racket of motorcycles and machines. You could hear it from blocks away, and it added to your excitement as you approached the fairgrounds.

Monday was always designated as Kids Day and admission to rides and sideshows was only a nickel until six o'clock. It was the day that youngsters had looked forward to since the spring, and the fairgrounds and midway were packed. It was probably the only day of the entire week that someone didn't try to sneak into the grounds . . . it wasn't worth the effort.

During the 1930's the rides weren't as sophisticated as they are now, but they still provided a lot of thrills. There was a ride called Crack the Whip, where you sat three to a seat and held on for dear life as you were shot across the lot and whipped back again. Another was called the Caterpillar, which was something like a small roller coaster, with a cover that opened and closed and gave the appearance of a caterpillar. Of course, the old standbys like the Ferris Wheel and the Merry-go-Round were there, and a ride we enjoyed most of all, the Bumper Cars. With one person to each car, you could drive in any direction and bump into whoever was in your way. Much like the drivers do in Victoria!

The first time you got up enough nerve to ride on the Ferris Wheel could be frightening. I can recall at six or seven, being petrified as I stared down at the ground and watched it drop away at an alarming rate. I was told to stare at the horizon, not to look straight down. Fortunately, it worked. The Starship was the scariest of all the rides. Shaped like an enormous rowboat, it held about forty passengers, and slowly rocked back and forth on its twenty-foot arm until it reached the top of its arc. Then you hung upside down for what seemed like an eternity, and everybody screamed. Older kids told us it was a good place to pick up loose change that had fallen from men's pockets while they hung upside down. But somebody always got there ahead of us and it didn't yield any more than the odd nickel and dime.

The gambling booths on the midway were, for the most part, con games designed to separate a man from his money. The games took a variety of forms, but had a common denominator — the scoring was so complicated and done so quickly, that the customer had to rely on the operator, and that was a big mistake. The booths either had numbered ping-pong balls, that floated in the air, or darts that were thrown at a numbered board. You got three tries for one dollar, and the score that you needed to win changed with each try. The game was skilfully controlled by the smooth-talking operator who kept putting your losses to one side, encouraging you to try "just one more time" to gain your losses back, and win a sterling (?) silver cigarette case. I have watched as people who couldn't afford it lost $20 or more in the space of five or ten minutes. A lot of money in those days!

The Penny Arcade was a popular tent on the midway. It was full of peep shows that cost from one penny to ten cents to view. The majority were western movies, a few comedies, and some of the first "girlie flicks." You placed your money in a slot, looked in a viewfinder, and when the lights came on you turned the handle to create the action. How fast the pictures moved depended on how fast your turned the handle. The average movie lasted about one minute.

Every once in a while you would hear shouting and laughter coming from in front of one of those booths where you threw darts at balloons, or hardballs at metal milk bottles, in order to win a stuffed animal. A crowd would soon be attracted by the noise, and they would see the lucky winner walking away with her huge, expensive Teddy Bear. Some of the new onlookers would try their hand at winning, and that was the reason for the exercise in the first place. You see, unknown to the spectators, the "big winner" was a midway employee, whose job it was to attract a crowd when business slacked off.

The sideshows were always fascinating. The Freak Show had the Fat

and Frozen Roadapples

Lady, who sat on two chairs as she answered questions from the audience; the Thin Man; the Alligator Man whose skin was supposedly like that of an alligator (it was, in all probability, a terrible case of psoriasis and he looked no more like an alligator than I did); the Man With No Arms who shaved his face with a razor held by his toes; and a man (you won't believe this) who pulled a member of the audience in a child's wagon, by means of clamps hooked under his lower eyelids! I remember how his eyes watered continually, and how miserable he looked. Freak shows were, in many ways, a callous exploitation of unfortunate people. On the other hand, it gave a good number of them a rare opportunity to work and to travel. They were held in high regard by show people, and often travelled in their own private rail car.

A sideshow featuring midgets was popular with midway fans. They usually had a musical variety program and, although their voices were often squeaky and the skits amateurish, the little people always put on a good show. A gimmick they featured during the show's intermission was to sell boxes of caramels, with prizes in some of the boxes. The candies weren't cheap, and a ringer in the crowd, early in the sale, would let everyone see the beautiful binoculars he got as a prize. Usually it was the only prize ever won, and the boxes contained a meagre six or seven caramels.

Undoubtedly, the most popular midway sideshow of all time had to be "Harlem in Havana," with twelve to fifteen topnotch musicians playing jazz, Cuban music and pop tunes of the day. They put on a terrific show, and their tent was crowded for each performance.

There was always a daredevil show, and ranking among the best over the years had to be the Globe of Death. It was a massive globe of steel mesh, probably twenty feet in diameter, with two motorcyclists inside who zoomed around and around, upside down and in opposite directions, narrowly missing each other. As part of the "come-on" in front of the sideshow, the bikes were mounted on horizontal steel rollers, that permitted bikers to ride the bikes at full speed. The roaring of the engines, and the hype of the barker, were calculated to get your attention.

One of the sideshows had a ramp with a slide at the top, not unlike a ski slide. A girl would walk a blindfolded horse up the ramp, mount it at the top, and plunge into a tank of water, approximately forty feet below.

Penny Candy, Bobskates

It was not only dangerous for the girl, but not much fun for the horse either. I suspect that the SPCA would prohibit such an act taking place today.

Barkers were a special breed and I used to love to listen to their well-rehearsed line of banter, always given at the top of their voices. I would stroll from one sideshow to the next to hear the various barkers. I always had to laugh when they invariably ended their spiel with the same line, "For the next two minutes, and the next two minutes only, I'm putting aside the roll of seventy-five cent tickets and you can buy admission to this fantastic show for the incredible price of only fifty cents." There were always people who rushed up to the ticket seller, to take advantage of the offer. It is doubtful that any tickets were ever sold for seventy-five cents.

One of the strangest sideshows that I remember seeing, one that really bothered me, was the show with the woman's decapitated body on display. She had several tubes sticking out of her neck, each one going to a container of life-sustaining fluid. The barker explained that she had been in an automobile accident, and a front-page story of the tragedy, in the *New York Times*, was framed on stage for everyone to see. Every few seconds her arms and legs would jerk spasmodically. It was, I learned later, a clever illusion done through the use of mirrors, but to a ten-year-old kid it was the real thing, and I used to stare at the body for minutes on end and wonder what would ever become of her. Months after the fair was long gone, I could still see that poor woman.

And there was, inevitably, a sideshow featuring something outlandish from deepest Africa. One year it was Wild Pygmies from the Congo. About ten of them were in the enclosure, and if you walked too close to the railing one or two of them would run towards you, screaming as loud as he could, and brandishing a stick with the obvious intent of impaling you. A neighbour told us that a friend, who delivered for the Hudson's Bay Company, took a parcel to the pygmies' living quarters early one morning, and they were shaving each other's heads and putting on tan makeup! Another childhood fantasy shattered.

Eating on the midway was always a special treat. There was something about the sizzling noise of frying burgers and hotdogs, the smell of onions cooking, and the hustle of the cooks, that made it so appealing. There were several eating concessions vying for your business.

and Frozen Roadapples

Most were run by "show people", with the largest (the only one with stools), run by the Chamber of Commerce or a service club, as a revenue producer. The latter always looked too clean for me; nice white aprons and spotless counters. The booths that travelled with the fair were more appealing because the cooks looked like they had slept in their clothes, and you felt like you were sort of "roughing" it to eat there. Shouts of, "Get your red hots here!" and "Best burgers this side of Boston," could be heard throughout the midway, and you made sure that you rationed your pocket money so that there would be enough left over for a snack. You also learned, through bitter experience, that you didn't eat just before going on a ride.

As I grew older my interests changed somewhat, and I became aware of the "girlie shows." By today's standards they were quite bland. . . tiny bras and G string, but nothing topless and, certainly, no nudity. One such show was called Artists and Models, and the barker's come-on was enough to excite the completely disinterested. You were herded into the tent like cattle, stood around (there weren't any seats) for probably twenty minutes, while the barker went through his "for the next two minutes only" routine, for as many times as it took to fill the tent. Finally, someone turned on a scratchy record player, and a scantily-clad "dancer" went through her routine. You suddenly realized two things: the girl had never taken a dancing lesson in her life, and, you had been had!

When you got tired from all the walking around in the hot sun, it was difficult to find a place where you could sit down, so many people grabbed a stool at the Bingo Booth. That way you could rest awhile under the booth's canvas canopy, and maybe win a dollar or two.

One afternoon in 1934, Don McRae and I were in the middle of the fairgrounds when it was hit by a twister. We fought our way to the grandstand where the horse races had been in progress, and watched through the gratings at the top, as the canvas tents were ripped apart, and light towers twisted and fell. One of the monkeys performing in an animal act was found a half mile from the scene, confused but in good shape. Fortunately, there were no serious injuries, but authorities said that if the roof of the grandstand had been facing into the twister, rather than away from it, it may well have lifted and dropped onto the hundreds of racing fans in attendance.

Penny Candy, Bobskates

Horse racing was, of course, a big part of Exhibition Week, but it didn't really hold much interest for youngsters.

I was most reluctant to include the following in my book because it is so bizarre I thought my credibility would be suspect. However, it is a part of our past, and it *is* true, because I witnessed it. Here's what happened. Spotted throughout the fairgrounds were small concessions, selling any number of gimmicky items. They usually consisted of a small table, one chair, and an improvised shelter of canvas, to protect the pitchman from the unrelenting sun. I watched in fascination, one day, as a chap regaled a handful of people with the following pitch: "What do you do when your knee is swollen? You take a pill or swallow some medicine. That's what you do. And where does the pill or the medicine go? To your stomach, that's where. Not to your knee, where it's needed." He followed the same line of 'logic' with headaches, sore shoulders, swollen legs, and so forth. And here comes the bizarre part. He was selling hypodermic needles, together with a bottle of 'special medicine,' for $2.50! You were instructed to inject the 'medicine' at the source of the problem, and to stop using medicines "that just go to the stomach." Frankly, at nine years of age, I was impressed. I wonder how many people suffered ill effects from that ridiculous home remedy?

Another huckster was the "weight guesser," whose sit-down scales were a regular fixture on the midway. "Guess your weight for fifty cents! No hands on the ladies!" . . . (his touching of the shoulder and hips was for men only). The prize was a cheap, black bamboo cane, with a kewpie doll attached. After watching him perform several days in a row, I judged that he guessed wrong about once out of every five guesses. He made a good living out of a small investment.

The Exhibition at night was quite different from the day time. The entire midway, rides, sideshows, and booths, was outlined in coloured lights, and big light standards made the whole place as bright as high noon. The major attraction, of course, was the evening Grandstand Show, featuring dancers, colourful costumes, comic sketches, and lots of music and singing. The grandstand was packed every evening for Saskatoon's best musical variety show of the year. It always ended with a spectacular fireworks display that kept youngsters on the edge of their seats.

and Frozen Roadapples

At midnight on Saturday, as the fair drew to a close, came the grand finale — the raffle draw for the brand new car from the revolving drum on the midway. Afterwards the fairgrounds quickly emptied and by 12:30 a.m. the roustabouts had played their last poker hand, as they started once again to pull everything down and get ready for the move to another city.

Yes, there's no doubt that Exhibition week was the highlight of the summer holidays for many years. I haven't been to a Saskatoon Exhibition for almost fifty years, and I am sure that, like the city, there have been so many changes I wouldn't recognize it. But I'm also sure it's as fascinating for today's youngsters as it was for us in the early 1930's.

Penny Candy, Bobskates

Penny Candy and Nickel Packs of Cigarettes

Sixty years ago the candy section in stores was unique. There has never been anything like it since. Every confectionary, and a few grocery and drug stores, had a special section with shelves loaded with penny candy. You could actually fill a small bag to the top with five cents' worth. The variety, especially to a five year old, was mind boggling. I can recall the patience (and, sometimes the lack of it) on the part of a busy store clerk who had to wait minutes on end, as a youngster tried to decide how to spend his few pennies.

You had to choose between sponge toffee; jaw breakers; chocolate maple buds; candy cigarettes with red tips; "black balls", which changed colour as you licked them; caramels; licorice whips; humbugs; gumballs; jujubes; and suckers of various shapes, sizes and colours.

And then there were intriguing items like wax false teeth; curved licorice pipes; licorice cigars; packages of flavoured sugar powder that you sucked up a straw; and miniature candy pop bottles filled with a few drops of grape, orange or lemonade. The best selection in our neighbourhood for penny candy was either Page's Drug Store and Soda Fountain on Victoria Avenue, or Barclay's Confectionary on Broadway. If your taste buds yearned for something more exotic, you could buy pieces of real licorice root and cinnamon bark for one penny at Stewart's Drug Store on Broadway Avenue. I don't recall that you could buy the

and Frozen Roadapples

latter in a candy store, so maybe they had been classified as herbs and could only be sold in a drug store. Another drug store item that was a real summertime favourite in our house were the ingredients to make ginger beer. There was nothing like a glass of cold ginger beer, with chipped ice in it, as a thirst quencher on a hot summer's day.

The most popular sellers, as far as boys were concerned, were the packages of flat, square bubble gum, each containing a card featuring the photograph and playing statistics of stars in the NHL, the NFL and major league baseball. You collected, by purchase or trade, as many as you could, until you had a complete team. One Babe Ruth card, Bill Dickey, or Lou Gehrig would trade for three cards of lesser known players.

Finally, as a major offering to your sweet tooth, you could blow the whole five cents on one chocolate bar, provided you could decide which one of the twenty on the counter you wanted. My favourite was the big, and I mean BIG, round, Cuban Lunch — milk chocolate, packed with peanuts. Today's chocolate bars are less than half the size of the bars we were able to buy for just a nickel.

When I was five years of age I took two shinplasters (twenty-five cent currency of the day) from my piggybank, and bought a huge marshmallow Easter bunny at Clarke's candy store. I was halfway through the bunny when Mother caught me, marched me down to the store, and told the lady she didn't appreciate her lack of discretion in selling it to me without a note from home. I suppose the incident would be comparable to a pre-schooler today going to a candy store with five dollars worth of change. A shinplaster was paper money, approximately half the size of a dollar bill. Originally minted in 1890, they were taken out of circulation in the mid-1930s.

The penny candy section in stores was sure a great place to spend time and money, and a real boon to dentistry about ten years down the road!

When boys grew into their early teens their interests changed, and candy eventually lost out to cigarettes. The transition went through various stages, until we reached the sophisticated level of custom-made packaged cigarettes. Early smoking sessions started with punk, that we found on the riverbank. Not just any punk would do. It had to be approximately the size of a cigarette, and be "a good draw". Shades of

Penny Candy, Bobskates

Tom Sawyer and Huck Finn! Punk soon gave way to the smoking of cornsilk, which was a more pleasant smoke, but, unfortunately, restricted to the fall of the year when corn was ripe for picking. If the tassel or cornsilk was green, it wasn't any good. It wasn't that we had discriminating tastes, it's just that you couldn't get it to light. If you were lucky, you would be able to scrounge proper cigarette papers from older friends, who were into "roll your own" smokes. Failing that, you went back to pieces of newspaper, your old standby. The difficulty with newspaper was that you had to make sure to smoke away from the wind. Otherwise, the smoke would get blown back into your lungs, and your chest felt like it was on fire. I regret to say that the stupidest thing we ever did, as far as smoking was concerned, was to smoke grocery string rolled up in newspaper! Now that was one wild smoke. I still blame my touch of bronchitis on that one.

It wasn't long before we got more sophisticated and began buying five-cent packages of either British Consols or Turrets, the only nickel packs available at the time. We would have to get someone sixteen years of age or older to buy them for us, or locate a small store whose owner was just scraping by and who overlooked the fact that your chin was hardly above the counter. My smoking cronies included Jimmy and Johnny Schmitz (the cornsilk came from their garden), George "Stevie" Stephenson, Stew Parr (the grocery string came from his uncle's Red and White store on Victoria Avenue), and Wayne Holmes. Wayne and I would get a nickel pack each and smoke the whole thing at one session, on the sloping banks behind Nutana Collegiate. At the end of one of those sessions the spots in front of my eyes were as big as bowling balls. Stevie was quite a character. School really didn't interest him too much and his marks often showed it, but he could go to a Laurel and Hardy movie and, one week later, repeat just about everything that was said and done. He was also one of those lucky people who could spend an hour or two with a musical instrument and finish by playing a tune.

Popular cigarette brands of the 1930's that come to mind include Old Gold, Players, Millbank, Sweet Caporal, Chesterfield, Vanity Fair, Camels, Raleighs, Athletes (that one didn't last long), and Lucky Strike. Remember L.S.M.F.T.? It was a highly publicized slogan at the time that the Lifebuoy soap foghorn was so popular. It stood for Lucky Strike

and Frozen Roadapples

Means Fine Tobacco. Millbank sales were quite high at one time, but they dropped dramatically when a news report claimed that several piles of horse manure had been discovered on the grounds of their manufacturing plant. Apparently the company experienced some difficulty in explaining why it was there, and customers soon switched to another brand. A story went the rounds that a tobacco buyer visiting the Millbank plant happened to see a worker mixing manure with tobacco. The embarrassed employee said, "I suppose you're going to cancel your orders now." To which the buyer replied, "Hell, no. That's the first time I ever knew there was tobacco in those cigarettes."

One of the best cigarette promotions of all time had to be the bridge cards gift scheme initiated by Turrets. The cards were approximately one inch by one and one-half inches in size, and one, two or three cards were contained in each package, depending on the size of the pack. The idea was to collect a complete decks of cards (all four suits), or try for a poker hand (a Royal Flush being the best). Gifts were awarded, ranging all the way from men's wallets to major appliances. The value of the gift depended on how good the poker hand was, or on how many complete decks of cards you were able to collect. It was such a popular promotion that a small store was opened on 2nd Avenue, where you could take your cards and pick up your gift. Just about everyone you knew was collecting and trading Turret bridge cards. I don't think there has been anything like it since.

Tobacco companies also did a great deal of radio and newspaper advertising. Two of the more popular radio programs of the '30s were the Lucky Strike Hit Parade, with Snooky Lansen and Dorothy Collins. She was replaced in a few years by Winnipeg's own Giselle McKenzie. The other major program was the Camel Caravan, with Benny Goodman and his orchestra, sponsored by Philip Morris. The program always opened with a midget bellhop, by the name of Johnny, who would yell in his high pitched voice, "CALL FOR PHILL . . . LLIP MORR . . . EESE". That's all that he did, but the program made him a well-known personality and earned him a bundle.

Every second or third summer, when we were kids, a rumour would spread like wildfire, that if you could find a printed number in the square that was under the Excise Stamp on the package of Sweet Caporals, you

Penny Candy, Bobskates

would win a bicycle. It was never true, but hour after hour, day after day, we would look in all the curbs, empty lots, and disposal containers for discarded packs of Sweet Caporals. It certainly helped to pass the time, and I imagine that is why we were always ready to believe the rumour the next time it came around. The same kind of rumour involved Player's cigarettes. If you collected a hundred logos of the sailor on the front cover, you were supposed to win a bicycle.

For years North American politicians have been saying, "What this country needs is a good five-cent cigar." Well, we had a number of them in the 1930's, one of the most popular being the White Owl. What politicians forget is the type of economy that generated a five-cent cigar. Surely they wouldn't want to go *that* route again.

When the smaller two-for-a-nickel cigars came on the market, Daily Double and Trump, we chose them over cigarettes. You felt just a little classier than the cigarette smoker. Real class, of course, came with the ten-cent cigar. I pilfered one from Mr. Parr's humidor and lit it up at a poker party. I soon lived to regret it. Within fifteen minutes I became pale, then sweaty, then green, and then quite ill. I paid the price for my indiscretion, and to this day — I can't stand the smell of cigar smoke.

Pipe smoking was the ultimate in sophistication. A corncob pipe was a must for beginners. When you tired of that, a classier type of pipe, like the popular Yellow Bole, or the fancy Briar, was called for. They appeared at about the same time as your first pair of white shoes, and both were chosen with the idea of impressing the girls. Today they would call it "being macho." Along with the fancy pipes came the scented tobacco, some with a fragrance so overpowering you were accused of wearing a cheap perfume.

Pipes came in all shapes and sizes and you soon became very much aware of which looked best for you. I preferred the long stem with a small bowl because my face was too small for the large bowl pipe. The latter, however, had the advantage of being the best bowl for borrowing tobacco. When a large bowl smoker took my tobacco pouch, it always felt as if it came back half empty. Actually, it was a good idea to own a large bowl, to use just for borrowing. A popular style with some was the Sherlock Holmes pipe, the kind that curled down over your bottom lip to your chin.

and Frozen Roadapples

I think most of us tried our hand at three or four different pipes over a period of a year or two before we gave it up. Personally, I couldn't stand the bitter taste of that glomp that always appeared in my mouth, no matter how many fancy filters I tried. The other problem was keeping the damn thing lit. You got fed up being on the receiving end of that old joke, "Slap him on the back. His pipe's gone out!"

Smoking was fun only because you weren't supposed to do it. Most of us quit as soon as our parents gave us permission to smoke at home. That took the fun out of it. We may have been stupid about some of the things that we smoked, but at least I was smart enough not to experiment with chewing tobacco. One of my friends tried it, accidentally swallowed some, and then thought he was going to die. He ended up in a couple of hours wishing he had!

Bobskates, Bobsleds and Frozen Roadapples

Winter had its own special smorgasbord of sports and things to do. When I was a kid the temperature used to hover between twenty and thirty degrees below zero for about four months, with snowdrifts high enough that we could toboggan off the roof of the house.

Weekends were taken up with snowball fights, road hockey, and skating either in the streets or on backyard rinks. Horses may have been vital to the city's economy but they also played an important role in road hockey. After all, most kids couldn't afford to buy a regulation hockey puck! We had a rule that was never questioned: "Don't open your mouth when you play goalie!" In mid-winter we called them "frozen roadapples," and at the start of the spring thaw they were known as "bran muffins." In either case, they were dangerous. Magazines were wrapped around your legs as shinguards. Building snow forts and snow men, and making "angels" in a drift, were all part of a prairie winter. As we got older, homemade bobsleds that held as many as six to eight kids would barrel down the riverbank onto the South Saskatchewan River. The hills near the sanatorium were ideal for both sliding and skiing.

Our house was heated by a coal furnace, and even the best Drumheller lump couldn't keep the house warm all night. You would wake up shivering about six every morning.

and Frozen Roadapples

It was about that time that the milkman would be hitching his horse to his wagon, to start his daily rounds. He would bundle up, with only his eyes exposed, as he trundled his heavy cases, loaded with freezing milk. When you rescued your delivery from the back doorstep around 7 a.m. the round cardboard stopper stood an inch or two from the top of the glass bottle, on its frozen cone of milk. Milk cost ten cents a quart and wasn't homogenized in those days. At Christmas you showed your appreciation for the rugged services provided by the mailman, the breadman, and the milkman by leaving a pack of cigarettes or a piece of Christmas cake at the door for pickup. Some residents, however, insisted that they drop in for a "wee drink," and on more than one occasion the sober and faithful horse finished the route, stopping at each house on the way back to the barn, as the not-so-sober deliveryman slept it off in the wagon.

Infectious diseases were also a part of the winter scene and included, at that time, scarlet fever, mumps, chicken pox, and whooping cough. Each illness was designated by its own coloured card that health authorities required you to place on the front of the house as a warning that people would enter at their own risk. When I had scarlet fever in 1931, a big, red card was nailed to the front door and the house was quarantined. My brother and sister went to live with my grandparents on University Drive, and my mother and I were left by ourselves for three weeks. Scarlet Fever gave our household its first coloured quarantine card. I somehow managed to accommodate most of the bugs that went around and collected quarantine cards like other kids did baseball cards. I suspect that if the Tasmanian Blight had passed through Saskatoon on an overnight stop, I probably would have got that too.

Among the major causes of death in the 1930's were pneumonia, tuberculosis and whooping cough. Development of the "wonder drugs," penicillin and sulphanilimides, practically eliminated those as a threat by the mid-1940's. The epidemic of Spanish influenza in 1918 claimed 250 lives in Saskatoon before it subsided. Flu shots did not appear on the health scene for some time.

A visit to the dentist was always made with a good deal of trepidation. I'm not implying that today's youngsters race to see who will get into the office first, but at least they have the advantage of a great many improvements in technique, equipment and medication. Fifty years ago the dentist had to operate the drill with a treadle, the kind that Grandma had on her old sewing machine. The faster his foot worked the treadle, the faster the drill went, and the louder the noise of metal grinding enamel. You had two choices of freezing. If the cavity was relatively small you could desensitize the gum by biting down on a piece of cotton soaked in novocaine. Major drilling called for the needle, that always appeared to be a foot long. If you chose the cotton swab (it was the cheaper freezing) and the cavity was larger than the dentist anticipated, you were stuck with desensitized gums that should have been frozen. And that could be painful.

Our family physician was Dr. McEwen, who lived in the brick house on the corner of Victoria Avenue and 11th Street, kitty-corner from Nutana Collegiate. He achieved considerable prominence when he literally put a teenage girl back together with silver wire, after she had been hit by a train while walking on the tracks near the Quaker Oats Mills. She had something like twenty-one broken bones, and the *Star-Phoenix* carried daily bulletins on her condition and Dr. McEwen's efforts to save her life. The whole city was caught up in the drama. She survived, and may very well be living there to this day.

Halloween was a fun night. Your costume was always planned well in advance, with a good deal of excitement and enthusiasm. It is classed, in my books, as a winter activity, because quite often we did our trick and treating in the snow. The festivities usually began that day with a class party at school, unless the night of witches and goblins came on a weekend, in which case the party was on the Friday. One of the boys in our class was absolutely petrified by grotesque masks, and his crying would be punctuated by screams, as he held tightly to the teacher's hand. It was really most unfortunate, and I often thought that he must have received a bad fright as a toddler, one Halloween, when he was confronted at the front door by a group of monsters. Doris and I made sure that the same thing never happened to our children.

Coming up with a costume was never a problem for me. My grandfather had an old bowler hat and a discarded cane, and I was Charlie Chaplin for eight years!

As we got a little older, the tricks became more important than the treats. Soaping windows was innocent fun, but we also made a dandy little gadget called "a screamer." You nicked the edges of an empty spool of thread, and wrapped it with about two feet of string. The idea was to place a pencil through the middle of the spool, hold it flush against a window, and pull on the string. The resulting noise was supposed to scare the daylights out of anyone inside the house. The few remaining outdoor johns were always in jeopardy at Halloween. Several were tipped over, sometimes when occupied.

One winter's day, when we were around eleven or twelve years of age, three of us were walking on the river ice between the Broadway and 25th Street bridges. This was definitely a no-no, because the previous year a youngster had fallen through the ice and almost drowned. We were a long ways from the warm water coming from the power plant, which made the ice treacherous on that side of the river, but we were still in forbidden territory. We had only been there a few minutes when we heard someone shouting at us from the riverbank about a block away. We couldn't make out who it was, nor was it clear what he was saying, so we responded by waving our arms and yelling something along the lines of "Drop dead." In ten minutes or so we tired of the ice and proceeded back up the riverbank to the street.

Who was waiting for us, but one of Saskatoon's finest in his full-length buffalo coat! He walked with the three of us to our respective homes and, in each case, chided the parents for their youngster's indiscretion. When we finally got to our house, Mother couldn't believe her eyes when she came to the door. Here was this mountain of a man (I came up to his knees) with her youngster in tow. The constable had written our names and addresses in his notebook, and when he read the names out loud Mother had a bird. As far as she was concerned, if my name was in that policeman's book, then I had a record. There was no way she was going to let him leave our house until my name was removed from that book. She pleaded, cajoled, chastised, until finally, realizing that he was in a no-win situation, he erased my name from the page. Mother then thanked him profusely for warning us about the danger of being on the ice, and promised him that I would never do that again. He left, probably wondering if he had made the right choice for a career.

I hated to have to go shopping in the summer months; summertime was meant for the outdoors. But in the fall and winter it was always a kick to go shopping at the Hudson's Bay store because I was fascinated at the way they made change for a purchase. Each department had wires that went to a cashier's cage, located on the balcony of the second floor. When you paid the salesclerk she placed the money, together with the invoice, in a metal cylinder approximately five inches long by two inches in diameter. She then pressed a button and the container shot up the wire to the cage, where change was placed in it for its return flight. It was fun to watch all those containers zip through the air, back and forth from the cashier to the various departments. McGowan's Ladies Wear, on 2nd Avenue, had the same system of making change.

Years later, when Eaton's opened their store, they introduced a machine in their shoe department that would show the bones of your foot, to ensure a perfect fit. It was a type of fluoroscopy and we used to stand in this thing for minutes on end, wriggling our toes and watching all the bones move. It was removed before too long as I believe it was considered dangerous. It's a wonder our toes hadn't dropped off long before then!

If you had reason to believe that your eyesight wasn't what it should be you went to Woolworth's or Kresge's, the original "five and dime" stores, to buy a pair of glasses. There was always a counter full of spectacles that had a variety of different lenses. I suppose that a few optometrists had already set up shop, and if there was such a thing as an ophthalmologist, only the well-to-do could afford his services. There were samples of reading material of various type faces, glued to pieces of cardboard, and you kept trying on glasses until you found a pair that improved your vision. You would have a time finding a pair that not only worked, but, also, that fit. If you did, you had a new pair of glasses for a couple of bucks. But you could forget about designer frames. They came in basic steel, plain.

Many confectionaries had a large weighing machine that didn't require a coin to operate. Unfortunately, the face of the scale was so large that everyone in the store knew what you weighed. I was so sensitive about being underweight that the only time I would step on the scale when anyone was around was in winter, when I wore a heavy coat. It made my weight a little more respectable.

There was one thing that we did as kids to while away the evening hours in winter, that was somewhat unusual and I don't know that the pastime has been as popular since. Girls and boys were really into French knitting! All that you needed was an empty spool of thread, with four shingle nails protruding from the top, and a ball of yarn. When the yarn was manipulated around the nails, a rope of finished knitting gradually emerged from the bottom of the spool. Girls usually fashioned a beret from the rope, and the boys would give it to their mothers to sew into placemats. The more ambitious types would knit a scarf.

When the Monday morning wash was hung on the clothesline in winter, the results could be quite hilarious. Frozen long underwear and trousers, blowing in the wind, were like some surrealistic ballet. Doing the laundry was considerably more tedious and tiring than what today's housewife has to contend with. That's when "Monday morning blues" really meant something. Dirty clothes were scrubbed by hand, as she bent over a washboard that had been placed in a tub of soapy water. It was backbreaking work. Then she rinsed the wash by hand, wringing each piece of soaking wet clothing over a tub. Finally, she hung the clothes out to dry.

The first invention that helped to take some of the drudgery out of washdays was the hand wringer, with its two rollers. A piece of wet wash was fed into the rollers, which were then turned by means of a handcrank, squeezing the water out of the clothing. The next major improvement was the introduction of the electric washing machine. Unfortunately, it proved to be a little too sophisticated for some women, who had washed all their lives in the old-fashioned way. My grandmother had the misfortune of getting her fingers caught between the automatic rollers. By the time my grandfather had rushed to the basement to turn the machine off, her arm had been drawn in almost up to the elbow. The early automatic shutoffs didn't always work. She sustained a painful injury that took several weeks to heal.

Broomball became a popular sport in the late '30s. It was played on ice with a soccer ball. The players wore rubbers and used a household broom, with half of the whisks chopped off, and a six-inch piece sawed off the handle. The rubbers, in theory, kept you from falling down, but only in theory. Public schools started to have broomball leagues. In our teens, curling was coming into its own, and with the availability of increased ice surfaces (like the Nutana Curling Rink) more and more high schools took up the sport.

Penny Candy, Bobskates

Occasionally, if it wasn't too bitterly cold for standing around, we would go to the ski jump in the university grounds on the riverbank near where the dam is now located, where local meets were held. It had to be the scariest, most rickety looking jump imaginable, and I couldn't believe anyone would want to climb to the top and jump. I saw several nasty falls, but I am not aware that anyone suffered a permanent injury.

The winter activity that was the most fun, and occupied the most time, was skating. Learning to skate started at four or five years of age, probably on bobskates, a twin-bladed skate that helped to maintain balance. You soon graduated to the conventional skate and struggled around the rink, with your ankles scraping the surface, for the better part of a season. Once your ankles strengthened, you were able to leave the security of the fence and venture to the centre of the rink, where the real skaters were.

Backyard rinks were common, with what seemed like at least one to a city block. In our neighbourhood the Schmitz' were among the first each winter to flood their backyard. It couldn't be done until there was enough snow to build a ridge that would retain the water and determine the size of the rink. Twice a week the surface would be scraped and the rink flooded with the garden hose. The neighbourhood's public rink was located on the grounds of Victoria School, where the city's Parks Department put up a portable five-foot wooden fence. There was a large ice surface for public skating, and a smaller one for hockey. The rinks were flooded by firemen from the hall across the street with big fire hoses.

When the streets became real slick it was possible to skate and play hockey on the road in front of your house, and sometimes skate to school in the morning, and back in the afternoon. Weather was seldom a deterrent. It could be 10 or 20 below with a 20 mph wind, but if you wanted to skate badly enough, you put on the warmest clothing you had, wrapped a scarf around your face and over your toque and earmuffs, and hobbled onto the ice. How we felt was probably best expressed in the words of that popular song (that no one seems to remember): "Oh, gee but it's nice to get back on the ice that I met you on . . . in Saskatoon, Saskatchewan."

Saskatoon had a number of semi-pro hockey teams over the years, with names like the "Maroons," the "Sheiks" and the popular and very

and Frozen Roadapples

successful "Quakers." The Crescent Rink was built downtown, east of the Traffic Bridge in 1927, and there was an indoor rink called the Stadium, at the entrance to the Exhibition grounds. The "Quakers" won the International Ice Federation Cup in both 1934 and 1937 and hockey enthusiasm was so intense that enough funds were raised by public subscription, at the height of the Depression, to build an artificial ice arena in 1937. One of the first games in the new rink featured the New York Rangers playing the New York Americans.

I watched a game in the exhibition rink in the early '30s when icing the puck was permitted when the teams were at full strength. It had the effect of making the game boring for the fans, and frustrating for the players. Another unique feature about our national game years ago was the sixth man on the ice, called the "rover," who lined up behind the centre man. This position was eliminated as unnecessary after a few years of trial.

Saskatoon and its environs has, over the years, produced several NHL players, some of them outstanding. "Newsy" Lalonde and the Cook brothers played on a city team in 1928, before achieving stardom with the NHL. A highlight of my life was having a beer in a downtown hotel after the war, with "Doc" Coutoure, Vic Lynn, Pat Lundy, and yes, Gordie Howe.

Two or three evenings each month during the winter when Bob Roberts and I were attending university together, we would go down to Picardy's on 2nd Avenue and have a hot chocolate, and the same thing always happened. For absolutely no rational reason we would start to laugh. We would egg each other on, until we were weak from laughing, and our hot chocolate was cold. How weird can you get? The waitresses would break up as soon as they saw us come in the door, because they knew what to expect. I doubt very much that Bob would admit that we used to do that. He is now vice-president for Coca Cola, based in Baltimore, Maryland. (Maybe that's why Pepsi is doing so well!)

Actually, that sort of strange phenomena had its origins years earlier, when Don McRae and I were chums. If it was the kind of day when there was absolutely nothing to do, we would have a laughing contest! We would start by forcing a laugh, until the real thing took over when you thought how stupid the other guy looked. Mother has come into my room when she heard this strange racket and actually found the two of us almost out on our feet, from several minutes of deep-down, no-stopping, face-contorting laughter. Don retired a few years ago as a Wing Commander. I wonder if he would have done as well had the air force known of his strange behaviour as a kid?

All of this talk about laughter reminds me of the time I went to the movies with a friend of mine, in our early teens. The movie was a real tear-jerker and we arrived at the theatre about twenty minutes from the end of the early show. That was too long to wait around for the second show so we decided to be seated. The theatre was as black as night, and after groping our way to two empty seats, we finally sat down. Unfortunately, I flattened a man's hat. Apparently he had become too involved in the movie to notice that his hatrack was in jeopardy. The hat was as flat as a pancake when I handed it to him. He wasn't too thrilled. I told my friend what had happened and he started to laugh, and I joined in. What made matters worse was that everyone on the screen was crying, and probably two-thirds of the audience was doing the same. When he stopped, I started. When I stopped, he started. The whole process was punctuated by a wave of intermittent, "SHHHHHH's," like air escaping from a tire. In a matter of minutes, we had ruined a mood that had taken the actors the greater part of two hours to create. When the theatre lights were turned on at the end of the movie, all eyes turned to the source of this most unwelcome interruption. The two of us felt like we had been caught stealing out of the poorbox.

A most unfortunate incident happened in the Capitol Theatre that same winter. A very prominent businessman, who was quite rotund (actually he was very fat) had unbuttoned the top button of his trousers, in order to be more comfortable. A lady, endeavouring to get past this formidable barrier, caught her dress on the man's zipper. Neither could move. She wanted to keep the tear in her frock to a minimum. He wished he had stayed home. The entire audience eventually got involved when an usherette shone her flashlight on them, to see what all the commotion was about. The unfortunate twosome had little choice. They shuffled up the aisle, joined one to the other, to the relative safety of the foyer. I doubt that he ever undid that top button of his trousers again. Even when he took them off.

and Frozen Roadapples

When we were around eighteen it was a big deal to buy a mickey at the liquor store. This was early in the war, before coupon rationing, but you were supposed to be twenty-one to buy liquor. That posed a problem, particularly when you were a young-looking eighteen. I was afraid that the liquor store clerk would make an example of me, by asking for my birth certificate, and then calling the police. So the buying of a bottle was quite an adventure in itself. I recall buying a bottle of scotch one winter's day, and when I got out of the store the bottle slipped from my grasp and broke. Jack Haver and Bob Roberts were with me. To this day Jack contends that we stood in mourning and shed a few tears! I don't recall that we did, but I do remember wondering if we could scoop the snow up with a shovel, and melt the whole thing through a sheet, thereby removing the pieces of glass and retrieving the watered-down scotch.

The difficulty we experienced as underaged customers was not nearly as difficult as imbibers went through a few years previously. The history of Saskatoon's "wets" versus "drys" is an interesting one. In 1910, the Saskatoon Brewing Co. defended its product as a "health food," and in local plebiscites held across the province in December, 1910, the "wets" prevailed in Saskatoon. The situation changed, however. A few years later in the Hub City prohibition forces were victorious by a whopping margin of ten to one, and even the government liquor stores were ordered to close. They reopened in 1925, and in 1935, beer parlours made their appearance, for men only.

Christmas, of course, has always been the most exciting time of year for kids. I'm not too sure that what we did was much different than what kids do today. The school and church concerts, the anticipation of Santa's visit, the unwrapping of presents, the gathering of family and friends for turkey dinner . . . all of these have been part of Christmas festivities for generations. I guess that the big difference between then and now was in the type and variety of toys on the market. Ours were generally made of wood or metal, and they certainly lacked the sophistication of today's Transformer Robots and Power Machines. One thing is for sure . . . our toys lasted longer. After all, wood and metal toys, and porcelain dolls, take a great deal more abuse than plastics. When my sons were young they played with a steel capgun that I had received for Christmas thirty years before! A popular game in the '30s

Penny Candy, Bobskates

was Snakes and Ladders, and the penchant little boys have for taking things apart and putting them back together, was answered with a set of Meccano. With the nuts and bolts, the screwdriver and wrench, and the pieces of metal, you could build all sorts of things, including bridges, battleships, houses and so on. Another popular item for boys was the "popgun," with the cork "bullet" attached to a string. Girls had their porcelain dolls, dolls' dresses, and little dresser sets. Raggedy Ann was the "Barbie" doll of the '30s.

Most kids collected *Big Little Books*, which featured a complete story, usually about a cowboy hero like Hopalong Cassidy, or comic strip characters like Dick Tracy and Tarzan of the Apes. The books were approximately three and one-half, by three inches, by one inch thick, and cost fifteen cents. You kept your favourites and traded the others with friends.

Our Christmas tree was always pine (I don't recall that customers had much choice), and because the living room was small and crowded with furniture, it had to be placed in the corner with the hot air register. Even though it sat in a container of water, the poor thing would soon start to shed its needles, and by the time we took it down on New Year's Day, it was looking quite bedraggled. The coloured tree lights were made so that when one went out they all went out, and it was often a frustrating experience trying to find, by trial and error, the bulb that was burned out. Families that used lighted candles for tree decorations were flirting with trouble, and more than one household had its Christmas ruined by a tragic fire.

A Christmas dinner that stands out in my mind was the one where we had one of those colourful baskets that you bought, full of trinkets, that was set in the middle of the table. A streamer from each trinket was threaded over the chandelier so that there was a streamer at each place setting. Before you started eating, each person would pull on their streamer, until the gift came out of the basket. It was a lot of fun, and quite exciting to see what each little "prize" was, as it was unwrapped.

Saskatoon was a perfect setting for Christmas, with mountains of snow, and clear starlit skies that were ideal for Santa's nocturnal visit. When you went to bed Christmas Eve, there wasn't any doubt that Santa would soon land his sleigh on your roof and slide down the chimney. The fact that the chimney seemed a little small didn't seem to matter.

and Frozen Roadapples

Prairie blizzards were unbelievable in their fury. The howling winds, gusting at forty to fifty miles an hour, blew the snow into drifts that were over your head, and swirled around houses, depositing snow into every nook and cranny. You didn't want to be caught far from home when one came, that was for sure. Visibility for drivers would be down to a few feet, and the steadily drifting snow could soon stall your vehicle, often with disastrous results. Motorists who stayed with their vehicle and left the engine running in order to provide some heat, were often asphyxiated when drifting snow plugged the exhaust pipe, forcing the carbon monoxide fumes into the car. Other motorists who left their cars and ventured into the storm to find the nearest farmhouse, often never made it. Visibility would be practically zero, and the numbing cold soon exhausted them. No matter what you did if you stalled, on a lonely stretch of highway, the odds against your survival in a winter blizzard were often insurmountable.

I was always intrigued by the patterns of frost that covered at least half of each window, particularly those facing north. You could draw pictures, and print your name, in frost that was up to half an inch thick.

I don't recall any bad hailstorms, although we had several of the garden-pea variety. A major storm that hit Richlea around 1931, where my Uncle Dave Wightman owned the general store and hardware, had stones the size of golfballs and broke almost every window in the district. That was the best year he ever had. A few years later the entire town was destroyed by a disastrous fire. Uncle Dave was a neat guy. He was a big, friendly Irishman, who worked hard and enjoyed life. He had served with the Medical Corps in WW1 as a "litter-bearer," the chap who goes out with a buddy, often under fire, to bring back a badly wounded soldier on a stretcher. A bullet had shattered his elbow, restricting the movement in his right arm. After the fire Uncle Dave, Aunt Olive, and their two children, headed for the West Coast, where he eventually opened up a hardware store on Granville Street in Vancouver. They lived on West 3rd Avenue, in Kitsilano, and when I visited them in February, 1948, he rousted me out of bed one night at two in the morning to attend a fire. Uncle was a fire engine chaser. He had been wakened by the clanging of several fire engines, and knew that it had to be a dandy. He was right. When we arrived at the scene it was the big Jericho blaze, that totally destroyed several WW2 barrack blocks and buildings.

Penny Candy, Bobskates

Each year during the spring thaw, we would stand on the Traffic Bridge and watch huge blocks of ice smash into the concrete supports. The rapidly moving ice gave the illusion that it was the bridge that was moving, and we would pretend that we were on a ship. It was great fun. One day we saw a small fawn that had been stranded on the ice when the river broke up. It looked scared to death and its fate was pretty much sealed.

I previously mentioned the making of "angels," and the fun of snowball fights. The other thing that little boys did in newly fallen snow was to write their names, as they slowly walked sideways. This required a degree of privacy, and a good deal of exercise before the name became legible. Come to think of it, it was not always little boys who tried snow-writing. Teenagers often held contests to see who could get their name and address completed before the tank ran dry.

When I referred to the public rink on the grounds of Victoria School, I forgot to mention the "change hut" that the Parks Department erected each year. It was partitioned down the middle to separate boys and girls, and had a potbellied stove. Youngsters took turns gathering in groups to bask in its warmth. When you took off your boots you made sure that you tied them together with the laces, and then placed them under the bench where you were seated. But that was no guarantee that they would be there when you came in from skating, particularly on those nights when older boys mixed them up by spreading them around the hut.

When the new artificial ice arena was built in 1937 it was, of course, the most popular place for skating, not only because of its large surface, but primarily because it was indoors. We went there quite regularly as teenagers and skated to music carried over the public address system. People normally skate counter-clockwise, but periodically the PA announcer would get everyone to change direction. Other times he would announce, "Boys only," and after three or four minutes, "Girls only," followed by, "Couples only." It was a thrill to circle the rink with a girl on your arm, taking long strides to the ever-popular "Skaters' Waltz."

The Hansleman family lived a few blocks from our house, somewhere near Melrose Avenue and 8th Street. They operated a large downtown meat market, bearing the family name, and raised St. Bernards as a hobby. In the winter, these big, beautiful dogs would be hitched to a sleigh and pull the Hansleman children around the block. I used to see them in the heat of summer and wondered how they ever survived.

A common sight on a winter's day, when you were on the riverbank in the vicinity of the sanatorium, was to see work crews sawing huge blocks of river ice. They were stored in an ice warehouse located near the Avenue H swimming pool, until the summer months. The ice was then delivered to residential and commercial customers in a horse-drawn wagon. The deliveryman would determine his customers' needs, mark his cut on a huge block of ice with a saw, and then chip off the required size with a large, sharp fork. The average home would take anywhere from a five to thirty pound block, depending on how hot the weather had been. It was from this weekly delivery by the "ice man" that we grabbed our coveted chip of ice when he was inside the customer's house. We would hold it with a handkerchief and lick it like an all-day sucker. It was a real treat on a hot day.

Some of winter's lessons were learned the hard way. Hitching sleighs to the family car was a popular winter sport until a fatal accident showed how dangerous this could be. When the car involved in the tragedy turned a corner, the sleigh, which was on a twenty-foot rope, swung into oncoming traffic. And no matter how many times your parents warned you never to touch metal objects with your bare hands, you had to try, just once, to see what it was like. And once was enough. Frosted metal held the skin fast, and the only way to let go was to leave some of it on the metal. One of the worst experiences of that nature, that I recall, happened to a friend of mine who caught his tongue when he licked the metal ice cube tray from his fridge. That hurt!

Winter clothing was interesting; bulk meant warmth. Some youngsters were so bundled up all they could do was waddle, and it was often a problem to find their faces. Farm families did their shopping from the Simpson's catalogue, which was relegated to the outdoor biffy when the new one arrived. The major clothing stores in the '30s that come to mind, other than the Bay and, latterly, Eaton's, include Caswell's, Gillespie's Big 22, Hearns, the Shirt & Hat Shop, and on the West Side, Adilman's.

Everything considered, it seems to me that winter was a great time of year when you were young, and an increasingly more difficult time as you grew older.

Entertainment

Entertainment in the '30s was much the same as today without, of course, the wonders of television. The radio was the source of most pleasure, and popular programs included "Amos and Andy," "Ma Perkins," "Gangbusters," "The Youngbloods of Beaver Bend," "The Adventures of Jimmy Allen," "One Man's Family," and the "Eddie Cantor Show." Radio's best dramatic program was the Lux Radio Theatre, hosted by Cecil B. deMille, and featuring prominent Hollywood stars. Today's popular "soaps" got their name from the late '30s and early '40s when daily quarter-hour radio programs, such as "Big Sister" and "Ma Perkins," were sponsored by Proctor and Gamble and Colgate-Palmolive.

A broadcast that was popular in our house in the '30s was Don McNeil's "Breakfast Club" that originated, if I recall correctly, in a prominent New York hotel. It was broadcast five mornings a week, in front of an audience of people having breakfast in the hotel dining room. The highlight each morning was a "march around the breakfast tables" led by the host, to the accompaniment of the hotel orchestra. It was a lively program that featured celebrity interviews, music and audience participation.

Singers of popular music, who achieved international recognition, included one of the most famous of all time, Rudy Vallee, known as the "American Troubador"; Al Jolson; Russ Columbo; Buddy Clarke, and Bing Crosby.

and Frozen Roadapples

In 1938 Orson Welles broadcast his famous "War of the Worlds" on American radio stations, and created panic in the hearts of thousands of listeners. The program purported to be an actual invasion from Mars, with on-the-spot coverage from reporters who were witness to the devastation and horror. Although disclaimers were carried in the broadcast, they were ignored by the great majority of listeners, who plugged the telephone lines of police, fire, newspapers and radio stations, throughout the country.

The recent death of Bert Pearl in Los Angeles at seventy-three years of age brought to mind the "Happy Gang," which was one of the most delightful, fun-filled programs ever produced on Canadian radio. What is truly remarkable is that it was on five days a week for twenty-two years, starting in 1937 and ending in 1959. The names of the originals were household words: Bert Pearl on piano; Blaine Mathe and his violin; Kay Stokes on the organ; Bob Farnon, trumpet; Cliff McKay, clarinet; Bert Niosi on the xylophone; and Eddie Allen, singer. Hugh Bartlett was the announcer until his tragic death from pneumonia. The program brought a great deal of pleasure to thousands of listeners, for more than two decades.

The other broadcast that held a special fascination for me as a youngster was "Hawaii Calls," produced by Webley Edwards and originating in Honolulu. When the snow was piled six feet deep and the temperature hovered around thirty below, I would listen to the surf pounding on the beach of Waikiki, as they played and sang those hauntingly beautiful Hawaiian melodies. It was my good fortune to visit Hawaii in 1970 and to sit in on a live broadcast from the Ilikai Hotel. When one of the lovely hula dancers threw a lei into the audience, and it landed on my lap, I thought I had died and gone to heaven.

Sports broadcasts that held you riveted to the set included the Joe Louis fights, with Clem McCarthy and then Don Dunphy calling the blow-by-blow, and Hockey Night in Canada with Foster Hewitt. Of course, that was the era of the six original NHL teams and most kids could name all of the players. During the intermission between periods we hung on every word as the members of the Hot Stove League commented on the game. The originals were Elmer Ferguson, Wes McKnight and Court Benson. The three star selection after the game, which continues to this day, was inspired by 3 Star Gas, one of the game's sponsors. Foster

Penny Candy, Bobskates

began each broadcast with "Hello Canada, and hockey fans in the United States and Newfoundland."

In 1936 Jesse Owens was sensational in the track and field events at the Olympic Games, and in 1938 Joe Louis knocked out Max Schmeling in the first round of their return bout. Other heavyweight contenders of the day were "Two-Ton" Tony Galento, who trained on beer and cigars; the Italian giant Primo Carnera; Abe Simon; Buddy Baer, and Ezzard Charles.

On April 12th, 1936, three coal miners were trapped for sixty-nine hours in what became known as the Moose River Mines Disaster. Families across Canada were grouped around the radio and were spellbound as they listened to J. Frank Willis report from the scene for the CBC. Two of the miners survived the ordeal. Other major news stories of the times included the birth of the Dionne quintuplets to an Ontario farm couple. The five little girls, and their attending physician Dr. Dafoe, became world famous but you hardly heard a word about the parents. Another baby made news headlines. He was the son of Charles Lindbergh, kidnapped for a ransom. The baby's body was found a few days after the kidnapping, and the world grieved with the parents.

The Saturday comics had syndicated strips no longer in existence, such as Maggie and Jiggs, Joe Palooka, Katz 'n' Jammer Kids, Barney Google, Alley Oop, and Gasoline Alley. Mutt and Jeff, by cartoonist Al Smith, was a popular feature, and became the oldest continuous comicstrip in the United States, running from 1907 to 1981. Al Smith died in November, 1986.

Talking pictures, known as "talkies" were introduced in 1930. The big movies of that year were "Hell's Angels" with Jean Harlow, and "All Quiet on the Western Front" starring Lew Ayres. Walt Disney's first major hit came in 1937 with a film that has proven to be a perennial favourite with adults and children alike, "Snow White and the Seven Dwarfs." The public wanted Disney to make a series of films that featured Dopey, but he always refused, saying that Dopey belonged with the other dwarfs. Other stars of the day were Douglas Fairbanks, Sr., Ronald Coleman, William Powell, Spencer Tracy, Franchot Tone, Claudette Colbert, and Myrna Loy. Boris Karloff became famous for his role in "Frankenstein" in 1931. In 1933 Fay Wray starred in "King

and Frozen Roadapples

Kong,'' and in 1937 young Freddy Bartholomew appeared in ''Captain Courageous.'' This was also the era of the spectacular Hollywood musicals. Dennis Morgan, handsome Irish tenor, starred in the ''Ziegfield Follies,'' and Fred Astaire and Ginger Rogers were paired in a number of movies that featured the music of Irving Berlin, Rodgers and Hammerstein, George and Ira Gershwin, and Jerome Kern.

Cowboy heroes were Hopalong Cassidy, Ken Maynard, and Tom Mix. William Boyd made sixty-six Hopalong Cassidy movies and became known as ''Hoppy'' to his thousands of fans. Gene Autry was the first of the movie's singing cowboys. Western singing stars included Wilf Carter, Ernest Tubbs and Hank Williams. The difficult times produced some of the world's greatest comedians: Harold Lloyd, Charlie Chaplin, Buster Keaton, the Keystone Cops, Eddie Cantor, George Burns and Gracie Allen, Laurel and Hardy, Edgar Bergen and Charlie McCarthy, Baby Snooks, Olsen and Johnson, the Ritz Brothers and the Marx Brothers. Many comics were recognized from expressions that became their trademark. For Baron Munchausen it was, ''Vus you dere, Charlie?'' Joe Penner was known for, ''Do you wanna buy a duck?'' Mae West had her sultry invitation, ''Come up and see me sometime,'' and Fanny Brice, as Baby Snooks, would confess, ''I've been a baaaaad little girl.''

Ed ''The Fire Chief'' Wynn was a popular comedian, whose program was sponsored by Texaco, and his nickname came about because of their Fire Chief gasoline. As a summer promotion, participating gas stations would give youngsters a red plastic fire helmet, when their dad got a fillup. They were a real popular item. Ed Wynn started up his own network in September 1933, in opposition to NBC and CBS. It folded by November, and he lost a bundle.

Favourite of all the youngsters was the loveable Our Gang with Buckwheat, Spanky, Alfalpha and Pete the dog. Most famous among the child stars was Shirley Temple. Others included Jackie Coogan, who appeared in movies with Charlie Chaplin; Jackie Cooper, and Mickey Rooney.

It's a little weird to list gangsters under the heading ''Entertainment,'' but the gangland hierarchy of the '30s received as much publicity in the news media as movie stars, and little boys were fascinated by the lurid details of their latest heists, and particularly, by

71

Penny Candy, Bobskates

their nicknames; "Pretty Boy" Floyd, "Baby Face" Nelson, "Machine Gun" Kelly, "Scarface" Al Capone, Bonnie and Clyde, and, one of the most notorious of all time, John Dillinger.

Mystery programs were popular in the '30s and two of the most successful were "The Green Hornet" and "The Shadow." The latter was always introduced with: "Who knows what evil lurks in the minds of men? The Shadow knows." The "Inner Sanctum" began with "Good evening friends of the squeaking door," and "The Whistler" was introduced with "I am the Whistler, and I know many things, for I travel by night." They were all good programs, each with a following of loyal fans.

Amateur hours captivated a large audience and the best of these for many years was "The Major Bowes Amateur Hour." Bowes introduced each program with: "The wheel of fortune spins round and round, and where it stops, nobody knows." Auditions for the program were held in major American cities, and the best performers were chosen to appear on the national radio program. Major Bowes had a gong which he clanged to cut a performance short whenever he felt the contestant was not up to his standards. (Perhaps that is where the recent TV "Gong Show" got its name.) Many of those appearing on the amateur hour went on to stardom in later years, including Arthur Godfrey, ventriloquist Edgar Bergen and his dummy, Charlie McCarthy, and comedian George Gobel. On September 8, 1935, a relative unknown sang on the program with a group called "The Hoboken Four." In a few short years he would achieve international stardom. His name was Frank Sinatra.

A very popular weekly radio broadcast for a great many years was "Amos 'n' Andy," which portrayed hilarious episodes in the lives of negroes, working and living in small-town America. Many listeners did not know that the characters, including Amos, Andy, Kingfish, and Madam Queen, were played by two white men, Freeman Godsen and Charles Correll. Lum 'n' Abner was another favourite program. The two characters ran a general store in Pine Ridge, Arkansas, and some people thought that it was the white man's version of Amos 'n Andy.

Roughshod but beloved, Wallace Beery starred in a number of "Tugboat Annie" movies, and perennial favourites, Mickey Rooney and Judy Garland, made several movies in the "Judge Hardy" series. Hollywood's most famous family was the Barrymores: Lionel, John and their sister, Ethel. Canadians who became prominent stars in the early

and Frozen Roadapples

days of Hollywood included Mary Pickford, Walter Pidgeon, Marie Dressler, Fay Wray, Norma Shearer, and a Mohawk Indian from the Six Nations Tribe in Brantford Ontario, named Henry Smith. His acting name was Jay Silverheels, and he became famous as the Lone Ranger's companion, Tonto.

Saskatoon had three theatres: The Capitol, The Daylight (across the street) and the Tivoli. One of Saskatoon's earliest theatres, the Victoria Theatre, was located on 2nd Avenue near 21st Street, and featured mostly cowboy movies. In later years the Roxy was built on the west side, a couple of blocks up from Adilman's Department Store.

Saturday morning kids' shows at the Daylight were always a treat, and you saved up your allowance to get the ten cents admission. If your parents gave you twenty-five cents to get a haircut, you would sneak off to the student barbers at Mohler's Barber School, for a fifteen-cent cut, and it was off to the show with the ten cents left in your pocket. It was those continuing serials that kept you coming back for more. Each week the hero, or heroine, in "Flash Gordon," or "The Mysteries of Dr. Foo," was about to be killed in some horrendous fashion, and you just had to get to next Saturday's show to see if he survived. In 1932 John Wayne, a relative unknown, starred in a serial titled, "The Shadow of the Eagles," and another popular serial, that started in 1933, featured Buster Crabbe in "Captain Gallant of the Foreign Legion." In the early 1940's the Dead End Kids had their own serial, "Junior G-Men."

Cartoons that were favourites with the kids included Popeye, with his skinny girlfriend Olive Oyl, and Wimpy who was addicted to hamburgers; Mickey Mouse, with Minnie and his dog Pluto; Steamboat Willie; and Betty Boop, known as the "Boop-Boop-Adoop" girl.

It was the era of innovative theatre promotions, as movie houses competed for the scarce entertainment dollar. Theatres often held give-away nights, when patrons received dishes or tea towels with their admission tickets. Colourful posters promoted the "coming attraction" in store windows, on the sides of buildings, and on fences and telephone poles. Anyone smart enough to save those posters can get as much as $500 each from today's collectors of Hollywood memorabilia.

In some ways I enjoyed watching the Movietone Newsreel almost as much as I did the cartoons. It was exciting to see something like a train accident, or major fire, actually take place on the screen. The fact that the news was at least ten days old didn't seem to matter.

Penny Candy, Bobskates

I'll never forget the thrill of going to the Capitol Theatre after it had opened in 1929, with its artificial sky installed. I would spend as much time looking at the sky, with its moving clouds and twinkling stars, as I would at the movie.

Saskatoon has had many outstanding musical artists over the years, and one of the youngest had to be Neil Chothem. In the mid-30s he was a classical pianist, a teenaged prodigy, who appeared in numerous concerts and on CBC radio, coast to coast. A few years later there was a very talented brother and sister piano team who received considerable prominence. Their names escape me, but I believe they were of Lebanese descent. They had a regular weekly broadcast on the CBC that originated in CFQC, announced by Wil Gilby.

Prior to most homes having a radio, the crystal set brought a lot of excitement into our lives. It was fairly easy to make. The parts included a cardboard coil wrapped in the fine copper wire from a Model "T" generator and coated with wax, a piece of crystal, a "cat's whisker" for the contact, and a set of earphones. Wires from the set were attached to either the bedsprings or a hot-air register, to serve as a ground. With luck you could pick up a local broadcast, usually a concert on the stage of the Capitol Theatre.

Most homes also had a gramophone and a collection of 78 rpm records. The Big Band era was in its heyday in our teen years, and I remember when Harry James, Spike Jones and Gene Krupa brought their bands to the city. If you wanted to jitter-bug you would put on a Woody Herman record, and if you wanted it more subdued you'd go for Wayne King the Waltz King, or Canada's own Glen Gray and his Casa Loma Orchestra. Orchestra leader Ben Bernie (never without his trademark, a cigar) would end each performance with ". . . and so this is Ben Bernie, saying au revoir, for all the lads in the band. Yowzah . . yowzah . . . yowzah."

To this day my favourite piece of music is still Glen Miller's "String of Pearls." It was also the era of the Zoot Suit, with its exaggerated wide shoulders, baggy pants and three-foot keychain.

America's favourite humourist and political satirist was Will Rogers. He was friend and confidant of presidents, cowboys, and the working man, and he would punctuate his jokes with a twirl of his lariat.

and Frozen Roadapples

He came to an untimely death in a plane crash in Alaska, piloted by his friend, world famous aviator Wiley Post.

There have been, of course, major changes made in the entertainment industry during the past half century. Not all of them, I am sorry to say, for the better. The most obvious has been the advent of television, an absolutely amazing medium that has, unfortunately, been prostituted to some extent. Television in the '30s was in its infancy and all programs were broadcast live, which meant that viewers could expect the unpredictable to appear on their black and white screens. Like the time when Betty Furness, a prominent TV personality, was selling a Westinghouse refrigerator. When she went to open the door to show the inside of this remarkable new product, she couldn't get it to open. So there she was, in full view of a nationwide audience, trying to sell a refrigerator with a door that didn't work. On another occasion an announcer had taken obvious pleasure in mixing a pile of fireplace ashes, bread crumbs, and other assorted rubbish, on a beautiful rug, in order to demonstrate the cleaning qualities of a new vacuum cleaner. He was more than slightly embarrassed when he turned on the switch and the cleaner failed to work. Someone had neglected to plug in the cord.

And live newscasts were not without their problems. One evening viewers were witness to an anchorman's nightmare. At the beginning of his news broadcast, the boom mike was lowered too quickly and too far. It struck him on the forehead. For the next two minutes he grimaced, as he tried to read the news through watering eyes. So much for the good old days of television.

The thing I miss most about the '30s is that great host of outstanding movie celebrities, whose acting abilities assured them longevity. After all, what young ''star'' of today can you name, who will be giving performances that Jimmy Stewart and Greer Garson are capable of, in their 80s? And what young comic of today will be commanding the popularity that Bob Hope, George Burns and Milton Berle still enjoy at their advanced ages? Many of today's stars seem to rise and fall in a matter of months, or, at the most, a few short years. Excessive exposure in movies, television and video cassettes, may be the reason.

Notwithstanding all of that, it's a marvellous age when you can sit down in the comfort of your own home, and watch an event of international significance as it actually takes place, a half a world away.

Penny Candy, Bobskates

School Daze

Public School

I started Grade 1 in 1929 and went to Victoria School for eight years. The first Victoria School was a one-room stone building that opened its doors when the village of Saskatoon was only five years old. A much larger three-storey brick building was constructed in 1909 to accommodate a growing population, and the original school was eventually moved to the campus of the University of Saskatchewan, where it stands to this day. Two major wings had been added prior to my arrival in 1929, and I believe the student body totalled close to 300 pupils.

What kind of impression do your first teachers have on you? Enough that I can remember all of them, by name.

From Grade 1 to 8 they were: Mrs. Marshall, Miss Esther Wright, Miss Daykin, Miss McDougall (she accidentally stepped on the class turtle!), Mrs. Mary Knowles, who taught Grades 5 and 6 (her singing classes garnered several awards at the annual music festival), Miss Wolfe, and finally, the school's principal, who also taught Grade 8, Mr. Hamilton.

We soon learned to behave whenever a substitute teacher by the name of Miss Prosser was on duty. She boxed your ears if you stepped out of line.

Mrs. Marshall had twenty-five to thirty Grade 1 students and I think she had the most difficult job in the whole school. That was particularly true in the wintertime when the uniform-of-the-day included a heavy

and Frozen Roadapples

coat, a scarf and toque, mittens and earmuffs, and galoshes. Not one kid was capable of dressing himself. She had to help you pull on your galoshes, button your coat, put on your earmuffs, and wrap your scarf around your face. She had to cope with that routine twice a day for at least three months of the year. You can imagine how much she dreaded the days that we could go out and play at recess! I remember that one day I had to sit on her lap as she frantically tugged at my galoshes, trying to get them on over my shoes. Finally, in desperation, she blurted: "Tell your mother to buy you a pair that fit!"

The Grade 1 desks were placed in a semi-circle, facing the blackboard. During the morning on our first day of school I was amazed to see one of the boys stand up and, very nonchalantly, have a whiz in the aisle. Mrs. Marshall was somewhat startled by the sight, but handled the incident in a most commendable manner. She apologized to the lad for not telling the class that we were to hold up our left hand when we felt a call of nature, and she would give permission to go to the bathroom. I don't recall that it caused any great commotion in the classroom, because I guess we were all thinking that we would have done the same thing, if the worst came to the worst. Mrs. Marshall then called on the school janitor, Mr. Carver, to bring his mop.

The whole school loved Mr. Carver, who had been the janitor for many, many years, and lived in the little house located on the corner of the schoolyard. He died two or three years after he retired, and the house was torn down. We were playing soccer one day at the lunch hour, and a boy broke his leg when another lad accidentally stepped on it. The stretcher the principal used to carry him into the school was the screen door from Mr. Carver's house.

Our school had an enormous three-storey cylindrical fire escape at the back. The first time your Grade 1 class was permitted to slide down the escape, after the regular Friday morning school assembly, you were scared stiff. You plunged into the darkness and hoped for the best. After that, it was fun. The doors at the bottom of the fire escape were spring loaded, and would open upon impact by the feet of the first person down. The principal always sent one of the bigger Grade 8 boys down the chute first, to make sure the doors opened properly. This was not always the fun that it would appear. The problem was that teenagers often worked their

Penny Candy, Bobskates

way to the middle of the fire escape on the weekends, and poured a bucket of water down the chute. By the time the Friday morning assembly rolled around the chute was covered in rust, and so was the first boy down.

Our Grade 1 class at Victoria School had been the first to experiment with the Winnetka System, whereby each student went ahead at their own speed, according to his or her own abilities. In other words, the class wasn't held to the level of the slow learner, where everyone proceeded from one lesson to the next. By the time we reached Grade 4 the very bright student was starting to forge ahead. It seems to me that Herbie Pinder was allowed to skip Grade 5 and then Grade 7. As a result, he was very young when he got into City Park Collegiate and, subsequently, university. Herbie and I had always placed either second or third in the 100-yard dash each summer, while competing in the school's annual track meet. The problem with jumping a year or two ahead in your schooling, he told me some years later, was that you were competing athletically, and socially, with boys two years your senior. I believe he felt, as a result, that he had lost out on a good deal of fun, particularly during his teenage years. I can recall Mother telling me that the Grade 4 teacher had said that I was being considered for mid-year promotion to Grade 5. "How would you like that?" Without a moment's hesitation, and with considerable feeling, I said: "No way. I'm not leaving my friends!" One of my smarter decisions.

In 1932, when I was in Grade 3, all of the public schools in the city went to 3rd Avenue United Church to see a slide presentation by Jack Miner. Mr. Miner was an outstanding naturalist who had started Canada's only bird sanctuary of any significance on several acres in Southern Ontario. Educators saw this as an excellent opportunity to teach children the importance of wildlife conservation, and of the increasing concerns about certain endangered species in both the bird and animal kingdoms. The event received a good deal of attention in the schools, in the weeks preceding Mr. Miner's arrival. So much so that we expected too much. I felt that the slide show was a big letdown. The church was packed; we were hot sitting for two hours in our winter clothing, and the black and white slides were uninspiring.

A major accomplishment in Grade 3 was learning to speak pig latin. Once you had mastered the technique of being bilingual you really felt quite grownup. The secret, of course, is to put the first letter of each word

78

and Frozen Roadapples

at the end of the word, and then add "ay". Thus pig latin becomes "igpay atinlay". It was strange, when you think about it, that not everyone was able to do it. You always made a point of speaking pig latin to them, just to add to their frustration.

When I was in Grade 4, I was chosen by my room teacher, Miss McDougall, to go to the university and take a type of intelligence quotient test in front of a class of education students. It wasn't because I was considered to be exceptionally bright. More than likely I was a good average, and therefore, represented most kids my age. The professor, a well-known educator by the name of Dr. Laycock, met me at the school and took me on the streetcar to the university. He was a big, friendly man, who walked me around the campus, explaining where the greystone was quarried in Saskatchewan and when the various buildings had been constructed. I was the only youngster to appear before the class for the one-hour test, and I remember being a little put off when I walked in front of the students and I heard one girl say, "Oh, isn't he cute!"

I guess it was around Grade 4 or 5, when I was really into reading, that Mom used to buy the Saturday edition of the *Chicago Herald*. It was a real treat and I looked forward to each weekend with a great deal of excitement. It seems to me that it had about seven separate sections to it, including terrific coloured comics. You could easily spend a couple of hours just looking at the photographs and reading various articles in such features as science, sports, Hollywood news, and, of course, the comics. Within a year or two I graduated from the *Chicago Herald* to a volume or two of *Boy's Own*, and a weekly paper called *Triumph*. Both were English publications that featured short stories about fighter pilots, bank robbers, boys' schools, and so on.

The first hobby that I remember getting interested in started in Grade 4. Mother gave me Dad's stamp collection, and I was really intrigued by the pictures on the foreign stamps; lions and tigers on stamps from India; the pyramids in Egypt; the Acropolis in Greece, and the canals of Venice on stamps from Italy. I would fantasize about travelling to those wonderfully mysterious countries, so many hundreds of miles away. Many of the stamps were placed in the albums with pieces of the envelope still attached, showing the postmark. That looked very untidy to me, and I couldn't understand why Dad would leave them like that. I immediately trimmed

Penny Candy, Bobskates

each stamp very carefully with scissors, and even cut off the perforated edges so that they looked neater in the album. Dad had been quite a serious philatelist, and I shudder to think of what I did to his collection.

Gordie Crewes (that spelling is probably wrong) was a friend of mine for the two or three years that he went to Victoria School. In July, 1928, he had been in a car with his parents that was in a collision with a train at the Lorne Avenue and Main Street crossing. His parents were killed, but seconds before the train struck, one of them threw Gordie out of the car window. He was being raised by his grandparents and we used to play snooker on his granddad's billiard table. His granddad rigged the light switch so that we had to put a dime in the slot, to make the connection so that the lights would go on. I thought it was about the smartest thing I had ever seen.

Bud Carson's father was a dentist and their house overlooked the river near the Broadway Bridge. They were the only family I knew that had a recreation room in their basement, and it was sure a great place to hang out when the weather was bad. I remember at one of his birthday parties we were playing "pin-the-tail-on-the-donkey." I could see under my blindfold but I wasn't letting on, because I was about the only one who hadn't won a prize. I lost when I hung the tail too low on the donkey's backside. How humiliating!

Herbie Pinder's twelfth birthday party was a wiener roast held under the first span of the 25th Street Bridge, supervised by his older sisters, Phyllis and Muriel. I thought it was great when his dad, the city's mayor, showed up for a while. I had never met a mayor before.

Creating "motion pictures" became the thing to do somewhere around Grade 5 or 6. You would draw a "stick man" in a running position on the corner of the last page of your scribbler. On each successive page you made slight changes in the position of his arms and legs. After approximately twenty drawings you ran the pages quickly, using the thumb and index finger of your left hand, and it gave the illusion of a man actually running. As you became more proficient you would draw two characters, possibly a dog chasing a cat. It was really quite fascinating. And it was the sort of thing you could do during a lesson, to make the teacher think you were really working.

School projects in the early years were a good way of maintaining a youngster's interest, and teaching him how to participate in a group. We

and Frozen Roadapples

always enjoyed our class project and looked forward to that part of the day when it was time to work on it. In Grade 1 we had to prepare a book of drawings of Holland, with each pupil contributing a coloured picture of a Dutch scene. It seems to me that they were nearly all windmills, dikes and tulips, with the more ambitious doing a drawing of people in their native dress. In Grade 2 we made a mountain out of cardboard boxes, that sat in one corner of the room, almost touching the ceiling. The corners were rounded with newspapers soaked in water (paper mache), and then the whole thing was covered in sheets of paper, on which we painted snow, trees, waterfalls, and so on. Our Grade 3 project was individual maps of the United States, made from a mixture of flour, water, and salt. When it had dried we painted in the forty-eight states, each in different shades of colours (light, medium and dark greens, browns, etc.). I wonder how many American school children ever made a map of Canada?

It was probably in Grade 3 that we started to paint with water colours and draw with pastel coloured chalk. I recall that the "magic" of colour combinations with paints fascinated me: yellow and red make orange; blue and red make purple; yellow and green make blue, and so on.

One year a magazine representative came to the schoolground just as classes were getting out to recruit sales people. This, from a school where the age range was six to thirteen years! You could sign for as many magazines as you thought you could sell, and were given the copies on the spot. I was in Grade 3, nine years of age, and took fifteen copies home with me. I had visions of embarking on a part-time sales career that would, at the very least, triple my weekly allowance. After half a dozen refusals from the neighbours I got discouraged, and lugged them all back to school the next day. Most youngsters did the same, and there were follow-up phone calls from disgruntled parents to the school principal. The sales rep apparently got into trouble with just about everyone involved, the parents, school authorities, and his boss. He had even given copies to youngsters in Grade 1. Other schools had similar experiences with overly zealous magazine representatives, until the distributors got their act together.

The first time as a youngster that I can remember being confronted with death was when my chum Billy died when we were in Grade 3. I am sure that I must have known some friend of my Mom's who had died, or read about a movie star who passed away, but Billy's loss was close to me

Penny Candy, Bobskates

and I recall being more or less baffled that a kid who was there one day was gone for good the next. He had gone to bed with a bad stomach ache and his mom did what most moms did at that time, she put a hot water bottle on his stomach to ease the pain. His appendix ruptured and he died within hours. It was hard for me to believe that I would never see this fun-loving kid again.

In Grade 8 five of us "published" our own weekly newspaper: Bud Carson, Wayne Holmes, Johnny George, Bill Arnott, and me. It sold for a nickel a copy. The news items were printed by hand with a special ink, and each page was pressed onto a jelly-like substance so that the ink was transferred to the surface of the jelly. A clean sheet of paper (8 1/2 by 11) was then pressed down on the jelly and the inked words appeared on the paper. One of the dads had suggested that we call the paper "The Sinn Finners," which had some Irish significance, but we really didn't know what. The printing process was so involved that the paper only lasted about three issues.

Boys in Grades 7 and 8 at Victoria and Buena Vista schools took their manual training at Albert School from a Mr. Ripley, a "no nonsense" type of teacher. After all, you certainly need discipline in a classroom full of young boys and sharp tools. It seems to me that just about every boy in Nutana gave his mother a wooden serving tray, with woven wicker sides, because that was the mandatory project in the first year. Individual projects became more sophisticated the following year, and some very respectable pieces of furniture were made by the more talented woodworkers.

In Grade 8 we played softball against a team at the provincial School for the Deaf, and after the game we were taken on a tour of the school and then entertained at a concert they put on for us. I was impressed by the bright, animated faces of the students, and astounded by the incredible noise in the hallways when some two hundred deaf students were changing classes.

Mr. Seymour Betts, an elderly gentleman, was a well-known choral director and voice coach in Saskatoon in the '30s. When I was twelve he offered free singing lessons to boys ages nine to thirteen. They were held one evening each week during November, in the school at the foot of the 25th Street Bridge. I decided to join the class, and when I look back on that long, cold walk in the dark of a winter's night, I can't believe that I was that fond of singing when I was a boy.

and Frozen Roadapples

When we were around fourteen, a chum and I tried our hands at being pen pals. We wrote to girls in the States whose names appeared on the "Pen Pal" page of a comic book. We thought it would be neat to have American girlfriends that we could con with all kinds of lies about how popular we were. In my first attempt I recall telling the girl how outstanding I was at track and field, and that I played the trumpet. Neither of us got a reply to our first letters, which took us down a peg or two. When we wrote to the next pair of names we had chosen, we were a little more conservative in describing ourselves. I corresponded for a time with "Bubby" Nagle, who lived in North Dakota. She sent me a photo in her drum majorette uniform and I was impressed. She later confessed it was a photo of her sister.

It is interesting to look back at my public school friends to see what they accomplished with their lives: bank vice-presidents, medical doctors, judges, physicists, millionaire entrepreneurs, Queen's Counsels, treasurers, vice-presidents of major industries, senior federal government officials, and one even became an army general. Many were war veterans who went to university on grants provided by the Department of Veterans Affairs. They were excellent students, mature beyond their years, full of incentive, and eager to make up for the lost time. For a generation that had grown up during a disastrous depression, and had played a major role in a catastrophic war, they had done exceedingly well. As far as the girls were concerned, the great majority went into marriage and the raising of children in the years immediately following high school graduation. But there were some schoolmates who managed to combine professional careers with marriage. Most were either graduate home economists or registered nurses.

High School

I entered Nutana Collegiate as a freshman in September, 1937. High schools held initiation ceremonies for their freshmen that were more fun than punishment, as was the case with several university fraternities. It seems to me that the boys had to wear their pant legs rolled up; their shirt tails on the outside, and carry books for seniors. Anyone accused of a misdemeanour was brought before a council who meted out punishment. I must have done something wrong, because I had to clean three flights of stairs with a toothbrush. When the war came along initiation rites were cancelled, as they were considered too frivolous for the time.

Scrap metal drives were held annually, when the entire student body had the day off to collect discarded metal objects. They were dumped in the schoolyard for pickup and eventual use in the war effort. One year, during the night, pranksters placed huge piles of bedsprings, tire rims, 45-gallon drums, hot water tanks and so on, in front of the school's two entrances so that no one could get in.

Nutana Collegiate is Saskatoon's oldest high school. It opened on January 1, 1909 with the name Saskatoon Collegiate Institute. It was renamed Nutana Collegiate in 1923 when Bedford Road Collegiate opened, because it was no longer considered appropriate to designate any one collegiate with the name Saskatoon. Its school colours of two shades of blue (known as the Double Blue) were chosen from the colours of Oxford and Cambridge, and represent truth and honour. No other school of its kind in western Canada can match Nutana Collegiate's "Memorial Art Gallery." Started after the first World War, it features paintings by Canadian artists that are dedicated to the memory of the many students killed in the war. The tradition was carried on following the conclusion of the Second World War. The works of art originally hung in the upstairs auditorium, but for some years now they have highlighted the main corridor and library. Featured Canadian artists include Ernest Linder and Allen Sapp. The gallery now proudly displays more than fifty paintings and some thirty woodcuts. It is considered an outstanding memorial, that encourages an interest in, and appreciation of, Canadian art.

In our first month at the collegiate the entire student body convened in the auditorium for a farewell to its retiring principal, Mr. Cameron. He was known as "Pussyfoot" Cameron to the students, because of his ability to sneak up on them without being heard, and catch them doing something they shouldn't be doing. He was succeeded by George Bonney, who remained principal for many years. The teaching staff included (some of the first names escape me): Titus and Dorret (English literature); Roxana Smith (French); Sexsmith and Morgan (Mathematics); "Squirt" Wilson (Physics); Reynolds and Garvie (Physical Training and Hygiene); Alvin Hamilton (History . . . in years to follow he became Canada's Minister of Agriculture with the Diefenbaker government); Thompson

and Frozen Roadapples

(home room teacher for "B" school); Dr. Wert (Biology); Irene Ayres (Latin); Ms. Shaw (History); and Murray Wilson (Chemistry).

It was in grade 9 that popping someone's fly open became so commonplace that some of the culprits developed it into an artform. Zippers had not yet been introduced to the male trouser, and the fly consisted of four buttons, with a fifth at the waist. You soon developed the dexterity of a professional pickpocket. And your timing was vital to your success. You learned to stalk your prey so that the strike was least expected, and the resulting embarrassment at its greatest. Like when he was in front of a group of girls, or on his way up to the blackboard. Your hand would dart out like a snake, and with any luck you'd pop all four buttons, sometimes all five. If a button or two flew off, so much the better. If you missed, or were sloppy in your attempt, you were humbled by your peers. This whole business became so bad that you developed a weird way of walking. If you were carrying school books you carried them over your fly, as a guard. When your hands were empty you walked in a half crouch, as though you were recovering from abdominal surgery. A stranger would think that half the male student body was recovering from appendectomies. As the hunted, you acquired the wariness of a jungle fighter. As the hunter, you developed the stealth of a cat burglar. Nowhere was considered out-of-bounds. The classrooms, the hallways, the campus . . . all became theatres of operation. I was standing at the blackboard one morning in Mr. Sexsmith's math class doing an assignment in front of the class with three other students. A girl came over to get the chalk brush from the ledge immediately in front of me. Instinctively, I jumped backwards a couple of feet and covered up. She was embarrassed . . . Sexsmith was angry . . . and I was confused by what had been a mock attack. Teachers soon clamped down on this juvenile horse play, and popping fly buttons disappeared as a school activity. But I have often thought of the fun we would have missed out on, if the zipper had replaced buttons by the time we were fifteen.

Inter-collegiate sports featured highly competitive leagues in boys' and girls' basketball teams in winter, and in football in the fall. Enthusiasm ran high on the part of the players and the student body. I used to watch the football team practice on the school campus on weekends. As a conditioning exercise, Clarence Garvie, the phys-ed

Penny Candy, Bobskates

instructor, would have the players carry one another piggyback and race halfway down the field. I would get tired just watching. How the guys survived I'll never know. I do know that the football helmet certainly didn't give the protection that the modern helmet does, and minor concussions were relatively common. Basketball was played in the new gymnasium, and enthusiasts could go at least one evening a week to watch senior "A" teams play, in both men's and women's leagues. Tennis was a popular sport with students, because the collegiate had, at that time, six tennis courts located at the back of the school on the banks that overlooked the city.

In Grade 11 I suffered the most humiliating experience of my entire life. Even more humiliating than the time, years later, when I emceed a show on the stage of the Royal Theatre, Victoria, with my fly open. Even more humiliating than the time, as a member of the chorus in "The Pirates of Penzance," I dropped my wooden scabbard that clattered on the floor, right in the middle of the soprano's solo. This mortifying incident couldn't have taken place in a worse scenario . . . the teacher was a very attractive single lady in her late twenties and a friend of my sister, which compounded the problem, and the class was two-thirds girls. It was in our third year Latin class. Here's what happened.

I was suffering from one of those niggling winter colds that never seem to go away, the kind that creates a tickling in the throat that makes you cough for minutes on end. My problem, on this particularly fateful morning, was that I was also plagued with vast quantities of intestinal gas. What happened should by now be quite apparent. Every time I coughed I broke wind. Gawd, but I broke wind. A devastating set of circumstances for which there was no apparent solution. I didn't have any lozenges to ease the tickling in my throat, and I daren't stand up to leave the room for fear of what other catastrophe might overwhelm me. Cough . . . BANG . . . cough . . .POW . . .cough . . .BANG. I would have given anything if I could have died on the spot. The snickers throughout the classroom grew louder. The teacher's face grew redder. In order to offset, if at all possible, the embarrassing sounds that followed each cough, I wrapped my feet around the legs of my desk and held on as tight as I could. This had the effect of raising the pitch of the offending noise, with a corresponding increase in the volume of the snickers. At this point I was beginning to lose what little control I had. It was two or three minutes of sheer hell. Finally I got rid of the tickling sensation, and about ninety per cent of the gas. I somehow managed to survive to the end of the class, but I could never look that teacher in the eye again. I dropped Latin.

I think that one of my classmates best summed up the whole disastrous episode, with the comment: "I thought I was taking Latin-3, but, because of Thompson, it turned out to be Farting-15!" In the weeks immediately following the incident I was greeted in the school corridors with rude noises. Most often these were created by cupping the left hand over the right armpit and vigorously pumping the right arm. Such was the price of fame.

Each year Nutana held an annual variety show, called "Lit Night," and every form in the collegiate had to contribute to the entertainment. The various acts included comedy skits, individual singing and dancing, and choral groups. The evening lasted over two hours; admission was fifteen cents at the door, and the auditorium was always packed.

In our senior years of high school, a group of us spent most Saturdays, and a good deal of our pocket money, playing pool in the basement of the Canada Building. The pool hall was operated by a Mr. Sugarman, and the group included Les Davey, Keith McColl, Stew Parr, Doug Smith, and Tom Dooley.

During our high school years we often went to a small hall near the exhibition grounds, where a four-piece band held forth on a Saturday night. The band was comprised of lads in their twenties, who were making a dollar or two by doing what they enjoyed most. The instruments included a piano, clarinet, fiddle, and accordion. Elmer Gordon, Budd Maggs and myself, and Beth McMorris, Madge Ingram and Francis Montgomery, would arrive at eight and leave at eleven, dancing every number. The "crowd" never exceeded twenty people, and one night we were the only ones there. The band, obviously, wasn't in any rush to open a Swiss bank account. It was a forty-five-minute walk, both ways, in the middle of winter, but it was our way of having fun. Today's teenagers would think we were crazy, but I wouldn't have traded our lifestyle for theirs, for anything.

As far as guys were concerned the one subject in high school that dominated most conversations, intruded on your thoughts numerous

Penny Candy, Bobskates

times daily, and created wild fantasies as you tossed sleeplessly, was s-e-x. Today's youth will find it hard to believe, but photos of topless beauties were difficult to come by and if, by the sheerest luck, you happened upon an overall full length nude photograph, you could demand almost anything from your peers, for a look. It was in high school that you learned from firsthand experience that "lover's nuts" was not a breakfast cereal. The malady inevitably struck around midnight, walking home from a date. The pain was real, the concern, grave. It was definitely not something you could discuss with a parent. Thankfully, a more experienced peer came to your rescue with a diagnosis, and a rather graphic description of its cure. At that point the "lonely vice" became a part of puberty.

The after-school hangouts for Nutana Collegiate students were Fyfe Smith's Drug Store on Victoria Avenue, and Pinder's Drugs, at Five Corners. Fyfe has to be credited for being among the first to recognize the need to fill teenagers' leisure time with something constructive. In the early 1940's he formed a boys' club from among the teenagers who hung around his soda fountain. They met in a basement room of Fyfe's store, and included Bob Berry, Walt Berry (not related), Eric Rigby, Wilf Wright and Jack Houston. Although there were only about ten members, President W. Thompson of the U. of S. was good enough to speak at one of the meetings. These astute gentleman recognized a growing need long before it became a popular concept.

A few short weeks following graduation from Nutana Collegiate in 1942, our summer holidays were saddened by a tragedy involving two lads who had been good friends of mine since Grade 1 in Victoria School. The two of them had been playing table tennis in the basement of one fellow's house on University Drive, when they made a mistake that would cost them their lives. They drank from what appeared to be a jug of homemade wine. If we had been with them that day, we would have done the same. In actual fact, the red coloured liquid was antifreeze that had been drained from the family car. They died within hours of one another. They had been inseparable in life. They were together in death. Their double funeral was held in Grace United Church on 10th Street.

One of our schoolmates received a fair amount of notoriety within months of graduating. He worked the night shift at the provincial stockyards on 11th Street, which is located a couple of blocks down the road from the Intercontinental Port Packers. Apparently, about three o'clock one morning, he ambled down to the packers and herded one of their cows back to the stockyards. He then made out an invoice at the going rate for beef on the hoof, and picked up a couple of hundred dollars. He was the first person in Saskatchewan in something like thirty years to be charged with cattle rustling, and spent a couple of years as a guest of the Prince Albert penitentiary.

I am absolutely amazed when I think of the number of fellows who joined up, that I knew as friends. All of them had lived in Nutana. The following is not a list of everyone who was in the armed forces from Nutana Collegiate, although they were all former students. It is a list of friends, many of whom I had known since childhood. I am sure there are also a few that I have forgotten: John and Jim Schmitz, Donald Munro, Jim Quinn, Nestor Page, Bud Ross, Vern Morrison, Wayne Holmes, Stan Nottingham, Bob Roberts, Ron Bailey, Vic Mandryk, Jim Greening, Jim Strachan, Ab Beazley, Bill Russell, Bob Hill, Tom Hill, George Mackie, Lloyd and Mickey Tomczak, Jim Smith, Jack Hall, Bob Grant, Jack Arrand, Jack O'Grady, Mert Zaphe, Bruce Parker, Bernard Wilkinson, Stewart Parr, Bob Taylor, Les Davey, Don Wheaton, Doug Smith, Keith McColl, Keith Laing, Bob England, Ted Sexsmith, Tom Dooley, Don Bergin, Don Thomson, Elmer Gordon, Con Fitzgerald, Bill Sanders, Jim McFadyen, Merril Lacheur, Cyril and Cormac Slough, Don McEwen and Willard Stewart. A few girls joined the services following high school graduation, but the only ones who come to mind are Dorothy George, Jean Neil, Ann Elder, and Betty and Ethel Harvey. If you combine this group of young people with similar groups throughout the entire city, you get some understanding of the vast number of lads, some still in their teens, who represented Saskatoon in the services.

The teachers at Nutana Collegiate were good, school spirit was high, and the memories are fond ones. The glow, however, is diminished by the thoughts of many bright, young men, who went to war, never to return.

Penny Candy, Bobskates

Bob Thomspon, announcer, writer, and then copy editor, at CJVI, Victoria, 1948 to 1952. The oversized microphone was "state of the art" at the time.

Staff announcers at CKRM, Regina, in 1946. Probably the only time in Canadian radio when three brothers (the Hills) were on the same station at the same time. Back row (l to r): Bill Walker, Harry Curtis, Tom Hill, the author, Sid Jacklin. Front row (l to r): Ren Graham (salesman), Grant Carson (sports), Jack Hill, Bob Hill.

Childhood friends strike a pose by the family car, as teenagers in 1942. (l to r): Tom "Doots" Dooley, the author, Stew "Soogie" Parr.

As senior citizens, they duplicate the earlier photo during their first reunion in 46 years, in 1989.

Farmers who couldn't afford gas or car maintenance removed the engine, added double-trees, and hitched up the horses. This strange vehicle was named after Canada's Prime Minister and called a "Bennett Buggy."

The Depression, with its "dust bowl" farmland, made it necessary for many families to pack up and look elsewhere for a livelihood.

and Frozen Roadapples

Yesteryear's police vehicles, a vast improvement over the horse and bicycle. Here we see a motorcycle with sidecar, a "squad car," and the "paddy wagon."

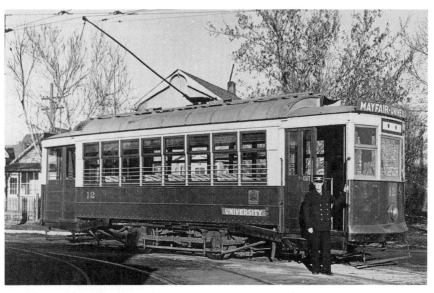

Trolley cars with wheels in the centre were known as "puddle jumpers" because they were easily rocked by students standing at the rear. Later models were larger, with wheels at the front and back.

Penny Candy, Bobskates

This parade of 1913 touring cars in downtown Saskatoon during the war was a sign of what the future held. However, horse-drawn deliveries of milk, bread, ice, groceries, and even water, continued through the 1930's.

By the 1940's the business district in most Canadian cities was taking on a new look with wide, paved streets; power lines; streetcar tracks; brick buildings; and parallel parking for the increasing number of automobiles.

Typical of the confectioneries of the era, this store featured a candy counter, a soda fountain, and seating accommodation. (Note the bananas hanging in the upper left of the photo, for splits and sundaes.)

A prominent district in many cities in the 1930's was "Chinatown," with its cafes, grocery stores, and laundries, where the washing and ironing was efficient and reasonable.

Teenage Courting

Something should be said about teenage courting in the '30s and '40s because it certainly was a big part of our growing-up years. But I'm not sure that I'm the one who should be saying it. Let's face it . . . I was an incredible nerd when it came to girls. The problem was kissing. I liked girls . . . I liked to be with girls. I liked going to dances and house parties. But saying "goodnight" at the door more or less petrified me. Made me unable to function. I never knew whether the girl wanted me to kiss her or not, and if she did, I sure as hell was going to let her down, because I never knew how to go about it. Do I grab her and kiss her? Should I ask permission? Should I just give her an "introductory" kiss on the cheek? Sometimes, as a last resort, I would say, "It's my birthday . . . are you going to kiss me?" . . . and the reply was always, "Oh, don't be silly. I know it's not your birthday".

It wasn't that I had never been kissed. One time I had an open mouth, full-on-the-lips, wet kiss that would easily rate a 9 on the Richter Scale. It had happened at Jean's fifteenth birthday party. We had some pretty ickey games at birthday parties, and this had to be one of the ickiest. But, by gawd, it got your blood pumping. Picture the following in the theatre of your mind. Three girls were picked to stand behind the sofa, representing Faith, Hope and Charity. The rest of the girls were allowed to stay in the livingroom, but the boys were herded out into the hall and the door was shut, so that you couldn't see what was taking place. You were taken into the room one at a time. When my turn came, I was already full of anticipation from all the giggling, guffawing and shouting that was going on. I was told to sit on the sofa in front of either Faith, Hope or Charity, and then I was to shut my eyes and I would be rewarded with a kiss. Gadzooks! Here were three of the prettiest girls in the school, and one of them was going to kiss me. The situation was getting to me. Nervous beads of perspiration ran down my brow, and my collar felt like it was choking me. Everyone in the room was yelling at me to sit down. The girls behind the sofa looked slightly embarrassed, but put up a brave front. There was no doubt in my mind where I wanted to sit, but I didn't want to make it too obvious. You pretended that it didn't really matter where you sat, but as you turned around to sit down you somehow managed to land exactly where you wanted to. And then SMACK . . . kissed by the school's most popular beauty. What a terrific birthday party!

And then it was my turn to watch, as another victim was ushered in to perform the ritual of the nonchalant but fully planned sitdown. And when he did, and shut his eyes, I was completely devastated by what happened. Popping up from behind the sofa was Jean's dad, later named "The Kisser," when Jean was around, and "Slobber Lips," when she wasn't. What a major disappointment! How humiliating! What a lousy game!

Another ickey game played at the party was called "Hit Your Head on the Ceiling and Jump." What the title lacked in sophistication it made up for in nonsense. As in the previous "Kiss" game, the boys were brought into the room one at a time. The first thing you noticed was that two of the huskier lads were holding each end of an eight-foot plank. A blindfold was placed over your eyes, you stepped onto the plank, the plank was raised until your head hit the ceiling . . . and at that point everyone in the room yelled "JUMP!" The sense of panic was overwhelming. You couldn't chicken out in front of your friends, but you didn't relish the thought of spending the rest of the summer with an arm or leg in a cast. You vacillated between forcing a smile, and almost throwing up. And then, finally, because there was really no alternative, and the yelling in the room to "jump" equalled in intensity and feeling that of the crowd at the guillotine during the French Revolution, you jumped. At this point you landed spread-eagled on the floor, and

Penny Candy, Bobskates

probably started the hernia that bothered you ten years later. You see, the problem was that the "ceiling" had been a book someone was holding, and the plank was all of six inches off the floor. Boy . . . I'll tell you . . . we had some pretty wild parties in the '30s.

The house parties held by teenagers took many forms and were really quite a bit of fun. In some cases anywhere from six to eight couples would take in an early movie, and then go back to the parents' house for sandwiches and dancing. "Deep Purple," "Blueberry Hill" and "Stardust" were popular dance selections at the time. In one instance, two mothers got together and rented a room in the YMCA that had a jukebox, as a combined party for their daughters. The jukebox had become a fixture in most cafes (now known as restaurants), and many weekly allowances went into playing selections of the Big Band era, starting with a nickel a tune, and soon progressing to a dime, and then a quarter. Apparently nickels started disappearing into jukeboxes long before we came on the scene. History records that the first nickel to be dropped in a jukebox slot took place on November 23, 1889 in the Palais Royale Saloon in San Francisco.

Player pianos, with their music rolls, were popular but expensive. It was fascinating to watch the keys move on their own as the piano played melodies of the day like, "He had to get out and get under, get out and get under, to fix up his automobile." I'll never forget how shocked I was when I approached my friend Jim Smith's house one day and through the livingroom window saw him tinkling the keys like the famous Carmen Cavellero. As far as I knew Jim couldn't play a note. I was even more surprised when he got up and walked away from the piano while the keys continued to dance up and down! Jim was a big, good-looking lad with a beautiful smile. He was killed two years later as a fighter pilot.

There were two or three surprise birthday parties in our teen years, until one was such a success parents decided not to have any more. Twenty of us were in a darkened livingroom, quiet enough to hear grass grow, when Helen, the fifteen-year-old guest of honour, entered. The shouted "SURPRISE" was so raucous she fainted. We didn't see her for the rest of the evening.

At house parties we danced to either the radio or the hand cranked gramophone. The latter was often the preference, because you could

and Frozen Roadapples

choose the music you wanted from the collection of 78s. The most popular orchestras for "cheek to cheek" dancing were Shep Fields and his "Rippling Rhythm"; Russ Morgan and his "Music in the Morgan Manner"; Wayne King the "Waltz King"; or "Swing and Sway" with Sammy Kaye.

Music lessons have been the bane of my existence. I've taken the piano twice, the guitar once, and I can't play a damned note. It's frustrating, because I love music, but I've always been defeated by my lack of patience. I don't want to practice, I want to play. I even took whistling lessons from a good friend, Bill Robinson, in my early teens. Bill was a natural, a la Al Hibbler with the Ted Weems orchestra, and he did his best to teach me. But the trick to a trill is in the curve of the tongue, and I just couldn't get my tongue to cooperate. Imagine flunking whistling? How depressing.

When I was thirteen I had jumped at the chance to learn to play the steel guitar. A door to door salesman was selling guitars and six free lessons for $12. I could see myself, a couple of years down the road, entertaining my girlfriend with the haunting strains of romantic Hawaiian melodies. It turned out that the lessons were given once a week, in a small room packed with about twenty students, most of whom had to stand. We took the guitar back.

House parties petered out in our middle teens, and our social life evolved around high school dances, dancing at the Art Academy and Cave Ballroom, going to the movies, or (because it was the cheapest), just hanging around at the girl's house. Some of the more popular downtown cafes became teenage hangouts, often to the owner's dismay. A 2nd Avenue cafe called the Silver Grey, was a great after-the-dance rendezvous, because it had booths with drapes that could be closed if "smooching" was on the menu.

We held a Sadie Hawkin's Day dance at Nutana Collegiate each year. A day originated by Al Capp in his "L'il Abner" comic strip. And that's where it should have stayed. As far as the guys were concerned Sadie Hawkin's Day was a disaster. Turnabout may be fair play, but the idea that the girls invited the boys out for an evening was less popular than measles. For one week of the year we had to go through the same waiting, wondering, hoping, and fear that girls went through before every dance

99

Penny Candy, Bobskates

and party. What if I'm not asked? What if I don't like who asks me? What if she looks like Cass Daley? (If you lived through the '40s you'll know who I mean, and appreciate the concern). What if she has two left feet? It was the what-ifs that gave you the sleepless nights. And then, when the big evening arrived, your date picked you up at your house, paid for the dance (every dance was "Ladies' Choice"), and paid for the soda after the dance. What an excruciating evening! If nothing else, Sadie Hawkin's Day made the boys appreciate the trauma that our social customs had foisted on girls, when it came to dating.

On New year's Eve we usually went to the Cave Ballroom, or to the function held in the Badminton Club, located near the Technical Collegiate. Sometimes we went stag, most of the time we took a girl, and all of the time we had a bottle. One of the New Year's dances at the Badminton Club was more memorable than most. During the midnight celebrating we tore down some of the green crepe paper streamers that were used as decoration, and wrapped them around our foreheads like a tennis player. The perspiration caused the green dye to run down our faces, and we looked pretty gross by two in the morning. I think the sight upset a few stomachs. I know that it did ours.

In Grade 11 we had an abortive attempt at making our own wine. It was our first, and last, experiment in brewing alcohol. The main problem was caused by the urgency for the bubbly. We were going to a mixed party the following evening and felt the need to be fortified. We collected a pailful of "Saskatoons" on the riverbank, mashed the berries, drained the juice, added our only bottle of beer for body, two quarts of water for volume, put in a cake of baker's yeast (we had never heard of brewer's yeast) . . . and let the concoction sit for a day to age. We drank the "wine" prior to going to the party. At about 10 o'clock severe bloating set in. Around midnight we felt like we were going into labour.

Mickeys of booze were quite common at our functions, but other than alcohol, we were not aware of anyone involved in the type of drug abuse that is so prevalent today. Marijuana, heroin, cocaine, and even glue sniffing, were things that you read about, but you never knew anyone who used them.

The automobile played a role in our teenage courting, but not nearly as prominently as with today's youth. Now, it is practically a must to have your own car when you get your licence. In my day it was a rarity to own a car. But there were exceptions. Lloyd Perry and Don Thomson purchased an old "touring" car (circa 1918) with a convertible roof that had three pedals on the floor, a gear shift and an emergency brake that were identical in appearance, a spark switch on the steering wheel, and a 10-cell dry battery that couldn't be replaced. It had to be hand cranked to start. It was quite a sight, and a lot of fun. Stew Parr borrowed his dad's 1930 Hudson on occasion, a huge car with a big trunk. His dad made a pretty thorough inspection of the car after Stew had used it, and it was the trunk that gave us away after an evening out. We thought we had cleared up all evidence of partying, but the circles on the trunk from the wet beer bottles did us in. No car for a month. When I was eighteen I got to use my grandfather's 1928 Pontiac (with the bronze Indian head radiator cap), because he was ill. The fun lasted until I failed to drain the water from the radiator one November evening, and ice was sticking through the block when I checked the car in the morning. End of car.

After a drenching rainstorm Ab Benesh would drive down Main Street in his dad's 1931 Chevrolet coupe with rumble seat, and spin two or three complete revolutions on the greasy clay road. The street was wide, not yet gravelled, and several years from having its present centre boulevard. Ab would also do figure eights, hoping he didn't hit the curb and snap the wooden spokes. It was fun to watch him, but when the ruts he created from his gyrations hardened in the sun, the road became difficult for cars and almost impossible for cyclists.

Whenever cars of that era refused to start, they had to be cranked. And that was hard work. The crank was kept in the toolbox on the runningboard, or in the trunk, and it fit into a hole at the front of the engine under the radiator. The eight pistons put up considerable resistance, and when there was a kick-back, the crank could break your thumb. To prevent such a painful and embarrassing accident ("How could you be so stupid?") you did not wrap your fingers and thumb around the handle as you would normally do; instead you placed the thumb on the same side as the fingers, so that it wasn't liable to get the full impact of a kick-back. There were two other rules to follow when cranking a car engine. You were well advised to have a friend in the driver's seat, who could step on the gas pedal as soon as the engine

Penny Candy, Bobskates

caught. And you were well advised to have a youngster handy to fetch the crank when you threw it fifty feet up the road. Cranking was a frustrating, no-fun experience.

Teenagers, then and now, set their own fashion trends. It was their way of saying that they wanted to be different. An expression of their growing independence. Fifty years ago teenage girls wore their cardigans buttoned down the back, "Sloppy Joe" full length sweaters, and full skirts with bobby socks. Footwear fashions included saddle shoes and penny loafers. The page boy hair styling was popular, and was often worn with a crocheted "snood." In their senior years in high school a few of the lucky ones were able to replace their cotton stockings with silk hose, but the war made the latter scarce, and pricey.

Boys wore pants called "strides," pork-pie hats (rounded crowns with a flat top), white shoes, and smoked pipes. The Zoot suit was the most flamboyant clothing craze of the '40s, but very few could afford to buy one. Hair styles were courtesy of the student barbers at Mohler's Barber School. During the war cuffs were never put on trousers because of the shortage of material. At one time pant legs were rolled up, exposing the ankles. Anything to be different.

For some reason nicknames were important during our teen years. If the gang hung a nickname on you, it meant that you were "in," that you were one of the boys. We had "Scoogie" . . . "Doots" . . . "Boob" (guess who?) . . . "Plug" . . . "Splinter" . . . "Barf" (don't ask why) . . . and "Stinky" (you know why). Nowadays, in some high school circles, it's pierced ears or a small tattoo that earns you the respect of your male peers.

In Grade 11 I got a terrific crush on a classmate and my life became a succession of peaks and valleys. Peaks, when she would go out with me, and valleys when she went out with other guys (which was most of the time). This was my second crush, and by far the worse. My first was in Grade 4 when I fell in love with the Grade 2 teacher. That was some romance. I would fantasize that big guys in Grade 8 were giving her a bad time in the school's basement, and I would come down and clean their clocks. That went on for the better part of a year, until the futility of the romance got the better of me. But this second infatuation was a real bone crusher. She was in my mind every waking hour, and I was completely and utterly hooked. I had been attracted, along with the majority of the male student body, by her terrific figure, pretty face, and bubbly personality. (She shall remain nameless — to protect the innocent.) I would go to her house and just sit and look at her. I was mesmerized by her presence and unable to function. It was kind of like Pee Wee Herman courting Raquel Welch. One lovely winter's evening, with a full moon casting a pale glow on the newly fallen snow, I walked up and down the street in front of her house, whistling popular love songs, for the better part of an hour. I was absolutely positive that she would see me and, overcome with affection, would either join me, or invite me inside. After whistling until my lips gave out, I decided to head for home. The only noticeable response to my efforts had been from several neighbours peering from behind their blinds. I had passed my girlfriend's house probably a dozen times, but I hadn't noticed that the porch windows were so frosted it was impossible for anyone inside to see anything!

As the weeks went by, my visits to her house became fewer, while the number of her suitors increased proportionately. My friends kept telling me how stupid I was. There appeared to be little that I could do, as our relationship went from cool to cold. I think that the depth of her feeling towards me can be best illustrated by what happened one evening. Her younger brother told me that she was going to be alone, so I was determined to make this the "night of nights." Somehow (although I wasn't sure exactly how) I was not going to leave her house until I got my first kiss. Ten months had been a helluva long wait. When she let me in, her blank expression indicated that maybe things weren't going to move too quickly. As I placed my hat, scarf and coat on the arm of the sofa, she left the room. After twenty minutes she returned with a kitchen chair, plunked it in the middle of the room, sat down, shut her eyes, and remained that way for what was probably fifteen minutes but seemed like a day and a half. On looking back, I think she might even have gone to sleep. I sensed that things were not going as I had hoped. This was not, by any definition, "making out." If she had been sending me a message, I'm afraid that it went over my head, because I rationalized that maybe her unusual behaviour was due to "that time of the month." Someone less sophisticated than myself probably wouldn't have understood.

One evening I had been invited over to her house and arrived in great anticipation. It was rare to be invited, usually I just dropped in . . . so I

Penny Candy, Bobskates

had great expectations. When I arrived it soon became apparent why the invitation had been extended. She was alone, alright, but her dad had left instructions for me to help a tow-truck operator get his stalled car to a downtown garage. When the truck came to the house (timed within minutes of my arrival) I noticed that she made no effort to get her coat on to come with us. "Aren't you coming?" . . . "Oh, no. I'm sorry. I have things to do." Great. Another evening of wild passion! It turned out that the trip to the garage was so weird, it almost made up for my disappointment. Her dad's car was going to be pushed, rather than towed, and the operator asked me to drive the tow-truck so that he could attempt to start the car while it was being shoved. A trickier piece of driving than mine would be . . . or so we thought.

As I climbed into the cab of the 1930 truck, it was a strange feeling, because the cab was high off the ground, and the seat was elevated, presumably to make it easier for the driver to get in and out. I found myself in a half-standing position, as opposed to the normal sitting down. The real fun began when I started the engine and put the truck into first gear. In a matter of seconds it became obvious that the gear shift had been broken and spliced at the break, which was about four inches from the floor. With the truck engine growling in first, I sat, in considerable bewilderment, waving the broken gearshift in thin air. By this time, the garage mechanic was waving frantically out of his window at me to speed things up. I proceeded to get down on the floor, with my head two feet below the windshield, and shift the stub of the gear into second. With a hasty look out of the windshield, to make sure I was still shoving the right car, I repeated the procedure to get into third. The entire process started all over again at each stop sign. I found the whole thing to be absolutely hilarious, and was cracking up each time I shifted gears. It seemed like I made about one-third of the entire trip on the floor of the cab.

I guess it was a little incident that took place some two weeks later that convinced me that the love of my life was not totally enamoured with me. Having been almost completely ignored for the greater part of a year, that possibility had weighed heavily on my mind. I had been walking home one evening, alone, when I saw her approaching me with an airman (she liked "older" men), their arms around each other's waist, her head leaning on his shoulder. This was definitely embarrassing. She was going

and Frozen Roadapples

to be shattered that I would see her like this. I decided, to help ease her pain, I would say "Hi," with a smile, to be followed by, "It's a lovely evening." The distance was now only two feet. She ignored me. To be honest, she looked right past me, as if I didn't exist. Another episode in the continuing saga of "The Great Teenage Romance." I think it was at this point I realized our chances of ever getting married were reasonably remote. The clincher . . . the last straw . . . the final blow, came a few weeks later. She had invited me to a house party being held by a girlfriend. I was euphoric. She had never asked me to go anywhere before. I had every reason to believe that our relationship had taken a 180 degree turn for the better. I was mistaken. You see, she invited me to go to the party and take another girl! While she was going to go with someone else. That was it . . . I mean, how much can a guy take? You may have to slam the door in my face ten times, but after the tenth time I ain't knocking no more. Enough is enough.

I became a survivor of a teenage crush. A crush typical of that endured by generations who had preceded me, and typical of that to be experienced by the generations to follow. The kind that turns your life upside down, lowers your school marks by at least two grades, reduces your appetite to the starvation level, and causes grave concern to your parents who, at times, suspect that you have become comatose. The kind of crush that you can laugh about years later, and, you'll be surprised to learn, continues to hold fond memories.

I was probably eighteen when I solved the mystery of how to kiss. A kiss, I found out, started with holding hands and looking into each other's eyes. The eyes said, "I like you. I think you're nice. I want to make this a special moment." Then you slowly moved your head towards hers, and gently placed your lips on her lips. And the lips said, "I respect you. I would like to see you again." No open mouth — no darting tongue — no unbridled passion. It was really so terribly simple, so very nice . . . and such a long time in coming. After that, I made up for lost time.

Kissing girls, or rather, not kissing girls, was only one of my problems as a teenager. The other was far more embarrassing, ten times more uncomfortable, and still plagues me on occasion. To put it in simple terms, without wishing to offend, I find it virtually impossible to function in the Men's Room when several strangers are there. Most of the

Penny Candy, Bobskates

washrooms in the theatres were small, with possibly only two urinals, and at the end of the movie the room would soon be so crowded it was like holding a party in a phone booth. Women don't understand the pressure that men perform under because they have individual cubicles. There was only one cubicle in the Men's Room and, although I never saw anyone go in or come out, it always sounded like a long-playing recording of Niagara Falls (music by I.P. Standing).

Now I know some of you are thinking, "What on earth has this to do with teenage courting?" While others are probably saying, "What in hell is he talking about?" Let me assure you that the problem of "lack of performance on demand" contributed to one of the most disastrous dates of my life. Here's what happened.

One summer when I was sixteen, a family moved into one of the two-storey homes on the corner of Victoria Avenue and 9th Street. There were two sisters, sixteen and eighteen, and they were very pretty girls. I somehow got the nerve to ask the younger one to a Saturday evening show at the Capitol Theatre. I think it featured Mickey Rooney in one of the Judge Hardy series of films. I was delighted when she accepted because that made me the first of the gang that hung around Fyfe Smith's Drugstore and Soda Fountain to date one of the sisters. When the movie was over, and we were leaving the foyer of the theatre, I asked her to please excuse me for a minute, and I proceeded to the restroom. Now, this in itself, is embarrassing to a sixteen-year-old, but that old saying is infallible: "When you gotta go, you gotta go." The room, as to be expected, was packed, My nightmare was just beginning. I gradually worked my way to the head of the line, took my position, feet astride, and waited . . . and waited . . and waited. My plumbing had seized, as I knew it would. With each passing moment the waiting became more unbearable, as I became increasingly aware of the fidgeting in the lineup behind me. I was becoming more tense as I knew that nothing was going to happen. So as casually as I was able, I zipped up, turned around, and strode nonchalantly past the lineup. I knew I was now going to be in deep trouble. Marg was marking time in the foyer, so I apologized for my delay, "I met a friend and we talked for a while" . . . and then we proceeded to the nearest cafe for the usual teenage dating treat, a milkshake! Milkshakes in the '30s were huge, and cost fifteen cents. The

and Frozen Roadapples

aluminum canister in which it was mixed was filled almost to the top, and one milkshake would fill three of those fountain style glasses. This, without a doubt, was not a smart move on my part. A sundae, yes, but a milkshake? No way. By the time Marg and I had walked down 2nd Avenue, over the Traffic Bridge, up the Short Hill, and the three or four blocks to her place, I was ready to burst. Marg may wonder to this day why I left her one-half block from her house, and made a beeline for the nearest back alley at breakneck speed. The only compensation for the entire evening was the overwhelming relief I felt, when I was finished. It was an incredible high. The pain was gone . . . the bad taste left my mouth . . . and I slept that night like a newborn babe. But I never went out with Marg again.

Some of the soda fountains in Saskatoon had punch boards, which were an extremely popular form of gambling fifty years ago. Lotteries were not available, and the Irish Sweepstake was the only chance the average person had of being rich, but the tickets were a little pricey (something like $1.50 a ticket). Punch boards only cost from 10 cents to $1 a chance, depending on the prizes the board had to offer. The average punch board was about eighteen inches square, with probably two hundred chances. You were given a small peg and you punched out a piece of paper, which you hoped would be a winner. When the board was sold out, it was full of holes and looked like a piece of pegboard.

I wouldn't want to give the impression that I represented the average teenaged Don Juan in the era of the late '30s and early '40s. Many of my male peers were more sophisticated and more aggressive in their courting. Some went in for heavy petting, and a few went "all the way." We learned that from all the bragging that took place after a date. Boys then as now were great at "kiss and tell," and explaining their conquests in detail was showing their "manliness." Girls had another name for it. But a teenage pregnancy was very rare. Unlike today, the stigma attached to the situation made life pretty unbearable for everyone involved. The term "illegitimate" became a social nightmare. It penalized for years to come the innocent victim of youthful indiscretion. Tremendous pressures were placed on unwed mothers by parents, churches, schools, and social agencies to give up their babies. The Salvation Army operated Bethany Hospital on Melrose Avenue for single girls who were pregnant. In its day

Penny Candy, Bobskates

it had been a rather stately, two-story brick mansion. The girls, from all over the province, were a curiosity to the neighbourhood, and often were subject to accusatory stares on their daily walks around the block. If I interpret today's teenage mores correctly from what I read and see on television, I get the distinct impression that a good percentage of youngsters in their early teens are engaging in love-making. In contrast, I would say that many of my friends eighteen to twenty years of age were virgins when they joined the armed forces, and a few, sad to say, were probably still that way when they were killed.

Growing up during the 1930's and early 1940's was fun. Growing up on the prairies was a plus. I feel, all things considered, that we had the best of both worlds. Unfortunately, that ended for many in the worst of all wars.

The Great Depression

I was six years of age when the stock market crash took place in 1929, and I have vivid impressions of what it was like as a youngster growing up in the Depression.

In 1935, Gerry McGeer, Mayor of Vancouver, read the riot act to a large gathering of unemployed in Victory Square, Vancouver. The mob had become unruly the previous day and had smashed windows in the Hudson's Bay store. Known for his booming voice, McGeer needed no public address system, or megaphone, to get his message across. When he finished, the gathering broke up peacefully. Undoubtedly, many of them took to riding in empty boxcars and headed east, where they thought they would be more effective with their protests, and also possibly find work.

Many of the unemployed, as they rode the rails across Canada, jumped from the train at the end of our street, just before it crossed the CN train bridge to the station where railway police were waiting. They would wander up the back lane, knocking on doors for odd jobs or something to eat. Mother could usually come up with a sandwich or two until it finally dawned on her that she was getting more than her share of transients. It turned out that they had a way of identifying a house to those who followed as being good for a handout, and the unmarked houses were no longer bothered. The signal was usually a chalk mark on a telephone pole or fence backing the house.

Penny Candy, Bobskates

I remember during the march on Ottawa seeing large groups of unemployed milling around the downtown streets, until the city fathers decided to set up a tent camp at the Exhibition Grounds, to house them. Approximately five hundred men were under canvas at the camp's peak, many of whom were sent to Dundurn to help build the army complex. An unfortunate incident took the life of a Mountie one day at the exhibition camp during a period of unrest. He was thrown to the ground when hit by a rock, and his foot caught in the stirrup as his horse panicked and dragged him around the camp.

Saskatoon wasn't as hard hit as many Canadian cities were when the market crashed, because farm crops were good and grain prices were up. An added boon to the city was the fact that several major construction projects were well underway, including the luxurious Bessborough Hotel, built by the CNR, which opened in 1935. Relief projects sponsored by the federal government included the 19th Street railway underpass, the nurses' residence at City Hospital, and a storm sewer system. The Broadway Bridge was also under construction in the early '30s. The 25th Street Bridge had opened in 1917, but city engineers prohibited the use of streetcars when the bridge was observed to tremble under their weight. The structural fault made the need for another crossing mandatory. It is interesting to note the major projects which were completed in advance of the depression. These included the Normal School (1923), the Sanatorium (1925), and the new Library on 3rd Avenue (1928).

The Bennett Buggy was a common sight in the '30s, particularly in farming communities. It was named after R.B. "Iron Heel" Bennett, Canada's prime minister during the Depression. Lacking the cash for either gasoline or much needed repairs, farmers lifted the motor out of the family car, attached a set of double-trees and a wagon tongue to the front bumper, and hitched up a team of horses.

The Depression also changed the face of prairie politics, when labour and agricultural groups got together to form the Farmer-Labour Group. They joined forces in 1932 with other movements to form the Cooperative Commonwealth Federation (CCF).

Reference to the City Hospital nurses' residence brought to mind an interesting piece of historical trivia that came to my attention when the original wing of the Royal Jubilee Hospital in Victoria, built in the late

110

and Frozen Roadapples

1800s, was being torn down to make room for a new addition. I received a phone call in my Ministry of Health office from George Masters, the hospital's administrator, asking me if I had time to come right out to the partially demolished building, and take a photograph of a curved corridor that had led from the original isolation ward to the rest of the hospital. I was fascinated when he explained his concern for getting a photo taken of the corridor before the building was completely destroyed. Apparently, in the 1800's, the medical profession thought that germs travelled in straight lines, and by curving the corridor the germs were prevented from getting into other areas of the hospital. Imagine. I guess they thought that they hit their heads on the wall and fell into piles on the floor. I've often wondered if Saskatoon's two major hospitals, built at the turn of the century, had curved corridors.

Finding employment was next to impossible. My brother, thirteen years my senior, could only find part-time work, two or three days out of each month, but his friend was a graduate engineer from the U of S and was more fortunate. He got a job delivering groceries for Tapley's Groceteria on Victoria Avenue, with a horse-drawn rig. Dennis Rivett worked for the Saskatoon water treatment plant from 1927 to 1971. He recalls that families on relief received monthly certificates which were to be redeemed in grocery stores for food, they were not cashable. The city's Relief Depot on 1st Avenue provided clothing, including men's long johns "that were so itchy people sold them for next to nothing." Many families found it impossible to pay the electric bill, so they would "jump" the meter with a piece of wire. If they were caught they were seldom prosecuted, because they couldn't pay any fine. Dennis played soccer with the Saskatoon Sons of England club, and in 1930 they lost to the Nanaimo team in the Dominion Championship semi-finals played in Winnipeg. The Nanaimo team had a number of good players from the United Kingdom, who worked in the Nanaimo coal mines, and they went on to win the finals in Toronto.

One summer Bert and a friend decided to ride the rods. This was probably around 1932 because I was nine or ten and sleeping alone in our tent in the backyard. They were gone about six weeks and got as far as Ontario. Bert arrived home one morning around five o'clock. Mother wasn't going to let him into the house at first because she didn't recognize

Penny Candy, Bobskates

him. He was filthy, had grown a beard and lost some weight. Bert never talked much about his experiences in riding boxcars, but I remember him telling me that they had been followed by a pack of wolves one time while they were walking along a railroad track in the Ontario bush. The only work they got were odd jobs, like washing windows, in return for a meal. There must be thousands of different stories by chaps who travelled across Canada in freight trains, chased by railway police at every station of any size. In the end, I think, it was a question of faraway hills looking green . . . but when you got there, they were all a dusty brown. If you rode the rods you were labelled a hobo . . . a term synonymous with the Depression.

Those who were innovative and ingenious could probably always make ends meet, somehow. Here is what a chap did, that I met in Victoria, who was in his twenties during the Depression. He and a friend went across Canada, touching all of the major cities, selling brooms over the phone from their hotel room for the CNIB. When they finally arrived in Montreal, almost one year later, they had saved enough money to finance an advertising promotion, which they sold as they wound their way back to the West Coast. They would find, in newspaper files and the reference library, something to be celebrated by the city they were in at the time. The anniversary of its incorporation, the birthdate of a prominent pioneer, the completion of a major building project, that type of thing. They would then purchase the middle page spread of the local weekend paper, and proceed to solicit local businessmen, most of whom were only too pleased to have their photograph, and caption, appear in the two pages of congratulatory messages. That trip would take the greater part of the second year. On their third trip, back to the East again, they purchased powdered household soap in bulk, and put it in small packages that they sold, door-to-door, as a new "miracle" household cleaner. At a profit of 300 per cent or more. He made a fortune after the war as a used car dealer. Figures!

Once a month, during the spring and summer, a chap with a thick European accent came door-to-door in our neighbourhood, buying used clothing. He was dressed in a shabby, ill-fitting suit and wore a bowler hat. When Mother answered the door he would grab her hand and kiss it, and then bow deeply from the waist. He paid next to nothing for the items of apparel, and sold them at an open-air auction each Saturday morning in the vicinity of the CPR station.

112

and Frozen Roadapples

Another sign of the times that I recall was the door-to-door character who paid cash for old gold. Money was hard to come by, so Mother showed him a gold watch that had belonged to my father. This chap set his scales up on our dining room table and proceeded with a flourish to place small counter-weights on one side until the scales balanced. He then paid cash, determined by the weight of the gold. I'm sure my mother didn't realize that the scales would be adjusted in his favour, or maybe she did, and just needed the money.

Before the Depression was over a great many families in Saskatoon would be on relief. Those lucky enough to find a job put in long hours for little money. Some worked twelve-hour days, six days a week, for as little as $40 a month. It may have been an interesting time to be a youngster, but it was an extremely difficult time for adults.

Penny Candy, Bobskates

Growing up on a Farm

You could argue inconclusively for a month of Sundays as to who had the most fun growing up, the city kid or the farm kid. Doris and I have done just that. She spent her childhood on the farm of her parents, Maude and Howard Dillabaugh, at Skull Creek, Saskatchewan. If you don't know where Skull Creek is, does it help to know that it's near Sidewood? Well, how about ten miles from either Piapot or Tompkins? Don't worry about it. The point is, Doris grew up on a farm, and here is her side of our argument:

Our two-hundred-acre wheat farm had a barn, a chicken house, an outhouse, a garage and a workshop. Farm equipment included a tractor and a combine, and the livestock consisted of five milking cows, a dozen chickens, three pigs and four horses, "Doc," "Skunk," "Floss" and "Minnie." Our farmhouse was a single-story, wood-frame building that contained four bedrooms, a large kitchen, a small living room and a "summer kitchen" in a lean-to at the back of the house. There was a trapdoor in the lean-to where we stored coal, potatoes and carrots. You think that putting on storm windows and thawing out frozen water-pipes was rough? Our house didn't have any electricity, running water or telephones. That's rough! We used kerosene lamps for light and pumped rain water from a cistern in the basement for washing. Drinking water came from the well. We lived in that house for eight years and thought it was great because everyone else lived the same way.

We didn't have the luxury on the farm that city kids do. That is, the luxury of lots of kids in the neighbourhood from whom you could pick and choose the ones you wanted to play with. Our nearest neighbour was two miles away. So it was nice having three older brothers — Laurie, and the twins, Keith and Ken (there was only six years' difference between the youngest and the oldest). We also had our farm chores to do, so we probably didn't have much free time to fill.

Horses have always been special to me ever since Dad gave me my own horse when I was six years of age. Dad gave him to me to ride to the schoolhouse because the three boys rode "Doc" and there wasn't any way he could carry a fourth. My horse's name was "Skunk," and he was smart enough that he would never run with me when I was tiny. He was black with a white blaze on his face and three white feet. One of my chores was to bring the cows in from the pasture each night for milking. I was too small to use a saddle, so I would climb up on part of the barn and jump onto his back, and off we'd go to collect the cows. As I got older, and "Skunk" knew that I could handle myself alright, he would race like the wind on our way home from school. I never used a whip on him and wouldn't let anyone else use one when they rode him. He was an even-tempered animal. We used to run under his belly when we were playing, and he wouldn't move a muscle. The only days we didn't ride the horses to school were those days in the summer when Dad needed them for farm work and in the winter when the snow was too deep for riding.

The Skull Creek School was a typical prairie schoolhouse: a single-storey, wood-frame building containing one large room with a potbellied stove and a cloakroom. Outbuildings included a barn for the students' horses and two toilets. Our teacher had twenty students and taught grades 1 to 8 in the same room. You learned to concentrate at an early age because you had to work on one subject while the teacher taught another to a different grade. The disadvantages of a one-room schoolhouse are fairly obvious, but it did give you the advantage of absorbing a little something from the teachings of the next grade, which probably made that year a little easier for you.

The schoolhouse was the centre of activity for the community. When there was a social function, everyone attended, young and old alike, and

Penny Candy, Bobskates

those who didn't dance would play whist. As the smaller children got tired, they would curl up on the coats in the cloakroom and sleep until it was time to head for home in the sleigh.

Gophers were a real problem at one time, and in an effort to reduce the population, Dad offered us a penny for every tail that we brought him. We would go out to the pasture, find a gopher hole (that was never a problem!), place a snare over the entrance and wait. When the unsuspecting gopher poked his head out, one of my brothers would give a quick yank on the snare, and two times out of three, we had made another penny. There were years when the grasshoppers were so bad that you could actually watch as they ate their way through a strip of wheat in a couple of hours, stopping when they got to the summer fallow and turning around for another feast.

One of the games we had on the farm was the "tire ride." It was made by looping a rope over the loft door of the barn, tying one end around a truck tire and leaving the other end free to pull on. I was about four when my brothers thought I was big enough for my first ride. What a thrill! I must have been fifteen feet in the air when Mother happened on the scene. The "tire ride" was grounded for a week.

The loft was a great place to play, particularly when it was raining. The boys made a boxing ring out of bales of hay, and they used to have "fun fights." The "fun" part stopped when somebody got a bloody nose or a bit of a mouse under the eye. The peak of the barn was another favourite place to play. We would jump off the peak onto a rack full of hay or slide down the roof onto the roof of the shed.

To help pass the time on a summer's day, we used to make canoes out of pea pods and float them in the horse trough. After removing the peas from a large pod, we inserted three pieces of matchstick or toothpick, the largest in the middle, to hold the sides apart. I guess city kids played the same game with woodchips and twigs in the water gushing down the curbs after a heavy rain.

Another summer pastime was to hunt for Indian arrowheads. We would wander over the bald prairies days on end without finding anything, and then we would strike a veritable treasure trove of a half dozen arrowheads or more. Experience taught us to scour the shoreline of dried alkali lakes and areas where the wind had blown the topsoil away

116

and exposed the hardpan. By the time we left the farm for Regina, we had quite a respectable collection of arrowheads of all shapes and sizes.

We had our own supply of fresh honey, which was a real treat. Uncle Alvie and Dad kept eight to ten hives on my uncle's farm. There is nothing as nice as eating fresh honey off the comb and then chewing the wax. Uncle Alvie always wore netting when working around the hives, but Dad never did, and the bees never bothered him. Alvie Murray was an MLA in the provincial legislature, representing the Gull Lake constituency. He died in 1946 during his second term in office, and Premier Tommy Douglas, together with several members of his cabinet, attended the funeral services in the tiny United Church in Tompkins.

Farmers were great at getting together for picnics and for holding local field days. Picnics were always highlighted by a pick-sides softball game with players of all ages taking part. I remember one time when a teenager broke his leg sliding into second base. The adults secured the limb by using a branch as a splint and tying it snug with dish towels. He was then placed in the back of a truck for a twenty-minute ride to the nearest hospital.

The small cactus that grows wild in the Prairies had a pretty red flower that develops into a fruit. It was considered a real treat. When an elderly British couple moved into the area, I scoured the countryside and filled a peanut butter pail with this special treat. I thought it would be a nice "welcome to the neighbourhood" for the new arrivals. Never having seen this strange-looking fruit before, the lady wasn't very impressed, and I was more than a little disappointed. She immediately realized her lack of tact and thanked me profusely "for whatever they are."

A real treat for kids was to search through the hopper of the combine for green kernels of wheat, which made excellent chewing gum.

When it was harvest time and the hopper was full of fresh grain, the truck would pull up to the combine, and a lever would release the grain into the truck. Then it was off to Sidewood to the grain elevators. Time was at a premium for the harvesters, who wanted to get the crop in as soon as possible before the weather took a turn for the worse. They couldn't take time off to come to the house for meals, so Mother would pack up the hot food in every pot and pan that she had and drive the truck out to where the crew was working. Men and horses worked from dawn to dusk, and at the end of each day, they would be covered from head to foot in dust with every muscle in their body aching.

Milk tasted special on the farm. After all, it couldn't be fresher, and there was lots of it. To keep it cool in the hot days of summer, we used to put it into a five-gallon pail with lid and lower it into the well until the bottom was sitting in the water. Farm kids had two or three glasses at every meal. We also kept the butter fresh that way. Eggs were kept fresh for weeks on end in a large, earthenware jar that was filled with waterglass.

Dad owned a Model T, but it was only used for trips to town because gas was too expensive to buy. When we visited neighbours or went for a Sunday outing, he would hitch up a team to the democrat. It was a rectangular box on four wheels with a front seat set on a pair of springs.

When Dad and the boys were clearing rocks off the land, he used a "stoneboat," which had runners made of two logs and a deck made of planking. When you are a farmer, you have to be a jack-of-all-trades, and Dad did all of his own repair work on the car and farm machinery. If it was something he couldn't handle, he took the part to a machine shop in Tompkins.

We had a community skating rink near the creek from which the area got its name. The men boarded-in a section of ground and then pumped in water from the creek for the ice surface. Kerosene lamps provided the light. They also built a small shack with benches that was heated by a woodstove. It was great fun to have skating parties and then make cocoa on the potbellied stove.

When the ice was rubbery on the slough near our house, we would walk and slide on it and defy it to break. It wasn't too serious if it did because it was only a couple of feet deep. When it froze fairly solid in the winter, we curled on it with "rocks" made from jam tins filled with concrete and bent wires for handles. In the summer we made a raft and pushed it around the slough with poles.

The roads were never ploughed in winter, so you went everywhere by sleigh. To keep warm in the frigid air, we heated flatirons on the kitchen stove, wrapped them in rags and placed them at our feet. Dad had a big, heavy cowhide he would wrap around us, but sometimes, no matter what you did or how much you wore, it was COLD.

and Frozen Roadapples

Digging tunnels in fifteen-foot drifts or making snow-forts was great fun for kids, but clearing pathways to the barn and the outbuildings was hard work.

The woodstove had to be on all day in the winter, and sometimes Mom would put a big kettle of buttermilk on the stove, add brown sugar and some butter and make delicious buttermilk soup.

Making our own butter on the farm was quite a performance. Dad would half-fill a churn with cream and then turn a crank that had two paddles on the end for the longest time until the cream turned into butter. The churn had a spigot in the bottom to allow excess moisture to run out. The butter was then packed into a wooden frame which had been dampened, and when you pushed on the handle, out popped your one-pound block of butter.

If Mom needed flour for baking, we would take some grain to the elevator where they ground it up and sacked it for us. Mom needed lots of it because she baked six loaves of bread every other day.

Christmas was just as exciting on the farm as it was in the city, and the Christmas concert in the schoolhouse was the social highlight of the season. Adults built a stage at the front of the classroom, and sheets were used as curtains. The students planned and rehearsed for the concert weeks in advance.

There was one concert that I remember quite vividly when I was five years of age. I had worn my new outfit, a lovely blue coat with imitation-fur collar and a matching tam. During the evening, small, yellow candles that illuminated the Christmas tree started a fire in the branches. My dad grabbed the closest thing at hand to snuff out the rapidly spreading blaze. It was my new coat. His quick action probably averted a tragedy in that crowded wooden schoolhouse, but I'll never forget how I felt when I saw my beautiful coat being used to snuff out the flames.

Christmas shopping was done from the Simpson's mail order catalogue, and when the box arrived, it was almost as exciting as Santa's visit.

We managed not too badly during the Depression because we always had our own eggs and poultry, and we could slaughter a pig or cow for meat. Farm families on "relief" received shipments from eastern Canada consisting of Ontario apples and cabbages and Nova Scotia salted cod and smoked herring. The cod was soaked overnight to remove the salt and then served up in a variety of ways: baked, fried, creamed and so on. Most farmers couldn't tolerate the smell of the smoked herring, so young lads used it as bait on their traplines for weasels, rabbits and the occasional coyote. The farmers' "Beef Ring" grew out of necessity and was typical of the cooperation found in rural communities. Neighbours would take turns donating a cow that was butchered, and the cuts were then distributed to the various farm families. The farmer donating the cow always got the heart, liver and choice of cuts. In winter the beef cuts would be buried under an outdoor pile of grain where they froze solid. For each hired hand that a farmer took on during the Depression, the federal government gave him $5 a month for the help's board and room and paid the hired hand $5 a month for his labour.

Whenever there was a local wedding, our town would hold what we called a "shiverie" (spelled phonetically because I do not know the correct spelling). It may have been a tradition unique to small towns because my friends who grew up in a city had never heard of such a thing. When the bride and groom returned to their home following a brief honeymoon, friends and neighbours would gather outside their house, shouting, singing and making a racket until such time as the newlyweds appeared at the door and invited them in for a social evening of food (provided by the guests), drink and music. That was a "shiverie."

You had to be tough to be a farmer. The hours were long, the days were hot, the work was demanding. And it was always a gamble. Grasshoppers, hail, drought, frost and rain at the wrong time, were your enemies. You were never sure until the grain was in the elevator. Dad and Mother celebrated their sixty-seventh wedding anniversary in a Victoria nursing home on March 25, 1987. They have since passed away.

I am quite sure that a kid growing up in the city had more to do and more places to go than we did on the farm. But I can tell you that I wouldn't have traded all of your candy stores, your movie houses, your parades or your sports events for my "Skunk." Unless you've owned your own horse as a youngster that you could ride to school, you'll never know what you've missed.

"What Did You Do in the War, Daddy?"

I am, quite frankly, embarrassed to write about my so-called "war service." I never heard a shot fired in anger, and my entire career lasted less than seven months. However, because no overseas veteran would have the temerity to write about his basic training in Canada, it may be worthwhile to record some of my experiences, depicting what life was like in the early months of training with the RCAF, under the highly successful British Commonwealth Air Training Plan. When my children asked me, "What did you do during the war, Daddy?" I had to reply, "I got as far east as Winnipeg and was discharged within seven months with kidney trouble." They only asked once.

I was sixteen when war was declared in September, 1939. It was a tremendously exciting time to be in your mid-teens. The massive German army soon outflanked the "impenetrable" Maginot Line, and they were overrunning all of France. "Blitzkrieg" was becoming a household word.

Bert had signed up as a passenger on one of the last freighters to leave Capetown, South Africa, for Canada and was on his way home within days of war being declared. His normal twenty-five-day voyage took something like forty-one days because of the zig-zagging to avoid German submarines. During that time they counted twenty-three allied freighters sunk by enemy action. Bert was a lieutenant in the Saskatoon Light Infantry, and he wanted to be in the 1st Division when it went

121

overseas, as his father had done in World War I. His alternative would have been to join a South African regiment, but it meant a great deal to him to emulate his father.

It wasn't too long before the school system had introduced army cadet training at the high school level. I don't recall that we had Sea Cadets or Air Force Cadets when I was at Nutana Collegiate in 1941. I think they came later. It was compulsory to take the training, and after a while, I volunteered to take an NCO's training course two nights a week at the downtown armoury. Not everyone who volunteered was chosen, so you felt like a big wheel if you were picked. We were instructed on how to drill a squad, and we all took turns giving orders. On the day of the final exercise, a senior NCO from the regular army came up from Regina to test us, and we each had to take a turn manoeuvring a squad through close-order marching drill. Some were lucky enough to get an easy drill, but I was given one that I don't understand to this day. When the NCO called me over and told me what he wanted me to do, I was stunned. It was a squad of forty students like myself, and by the time I was finished with them, they were facing in eighteen different directions. We had been told that a cardinal sin of drilling men was to lose control, and that whatever happened, always keep giving orders. So I was firing off orders as quickly as I could think of them, and the squad wound up all over the bloody parade square with half of them doubled up laughing. It was a relief that it was the last training session of the year.

When I was eighteen and had graduated from Nutana Collegiate, I decided to give university a go. Most of my friends were going, and I had always looked forward to being a varsity student. A few of our friends had already joined up. The minimum age was down to seventeen-and-a-half. France had long since been conquered. England was being bombed regularly . . . the States still wasn't in it . . . and Germany was talking of invading Britain. The government would permit you to go to university, but if you failed any courses, you had to drop out and make yourself available for the draft. Bob Roberts and I made a pact that we would go for just one year, and at the end of that year we would join the airforce.

We were required to take COTC training at university two nights a week and had been issued a private's uniform. Wearing it back and forth

and Frozen Roadapples

to the university was a macho feeling. We wore white flashes in our caps to show that we were officer cadets, and regular service personnel were supposed to salute us, but I don't recall that anyone every did. They knew that we were college students and couldn't have cared less about us. Who could blame them?

I quit in April, a few weeks before the finals, because my chances of passing on a scale of one to ten were about minus three. I didn't even have some of the textbooks.

I went down to the RCAF recruiting office with a good friend of mine whose dad had talked him into joining the ground crew and becoming an airframe mechanic, or whatever was available. I did the same because I didn't think I had a prayer of passing the aircrew physical. I was several pounds underweight and had suffered from chronic nephritis for a year at seventeen years of age. It apparently was a hangover from having scarlet fever as a kid. It was a serious kidney condition, and although I wasn't going to tell the doctor about it, I just didn't see myself as pilot material. I had been told that, having had chronic nephritis within eighteen months of joining up, I would be classified as ''4F'' (unfit for service). However, at the recruiting station, they had an officer from the First World War flying corps whose job it was to talk recruits into joining aircrew. The Allies had suffered heavy losses in air battles, and they needed all the aircrew they could get for the British Commonwealth Air Training Plan. He asked me why I wasn't joining aircrew, and I told him that I wanted to, that I felt I would be a good pilot, but I thought I would be too skinny. He checked with the doctor, who confirmed I was about twelve pounds under the minimal requirement for the forces. Most of my friends were aircrew recruits, and I didn't want this chance to slip away. I told the doctor that our family was all skinny, that my grandfather had weighed about 110 pounds, and I said my Mother didn't weigh more than ninety pounds wringing wet. They decided to give me two months to put on some weight. I always had a big appetite, so the only thing I could figure may help was to eat a brick of ice cream and bananas nearly every night before going to bed. In two months I put on four pounds and almost ruined my stomach. The doctor misrepresented my weight on the enlistment form, and I was sworn into the RCAF (aircrew) on June 1, 1943, my twentieth birthday.

Penny Candy, Bobskates

What I had done to bluff my way in was no big deal. Many lads were too young and lied about their age; others had operations at their own expense in order to pass the medical. It was because just about everyone you knew was in the service, and you wanted to be with them.

I was told to report to Manning Depot at Edmonton on August 10, and was given a little red, white and blue button in my lapel to show that I was a member of the Air Force. It was readily recognizable at that point in the war, and you were proud to wear it.

By this time the rationing of food, gasoline and liquor was pretty much a part of everyday living. Tuesdays and Fridays had been declared "meatless days" by the federal government. Shipyards and war factories were on twenty-four-hour production, and music was broadcast throughout the workplace in order to improve employee efficiency. Women worked side by side with men on the assembly lines and, for the first time, received equal pay for equal work. "Rosie the Riveter," taken from a popular song of the same name, became a symbol of the times. Everybody was either singing, humming or whistling "The White Cliffs of Dover," introduced by the English singing star Vera Lynn in 1942. War Bond drives were held regularly, with Hollywood celebrities playing a major role in the States. Jack Benny auctioned off one of his violins for one million dollars worth of bonds during a celebrity auction. He told the press the violin only cost him $75. Members of the armed forces were encouraged to buy bonds, and when an instalment was deducted from a private's pay of $39 a month, it didn't leave much for entertainment. "Victory Gardens" appeared in vacant lots and anywhere else that vegetables would grow, and "V for Victory" became a slogan that was on everyone's lips, scrawled on walls and fences, and printed on posters, in magazines and newspapers. I am unaware of its origins, but it received international recognition as a morale booster when Winston Churchill raised two fingers in a "V for Victory" salute on every public occasion, sometimes using both hands.

A major attraction during the war years, and the city's cheapest form of entertainment, was to load up the car with the family and drive out to the No. 4 Service Flying Training School at the airport to watch student pilots learn to fly. Every weekend, particularly Sunday afternoons, dozens of cars would parallel park along the shoulder of the gravelled

and Frozen Roadapples

highway. The SFTS featured twin-engined Avro Ansons, the flying classroom for training bomber pilots. Fighter pilots were trained in single engined Harvard trainers. The thing that made it so exciting was the student who had obvious problems with depth perception. Some tried to land their plane fifteen to twenty feet above the runway, and others tried to land three feet under the runway. The latter provided the most thrills. The plane's landing gear would slam the tarmac with a thud, causing the plane to bounce fifteen to thirty feet straight up. The height of the bounce depended entirely on the force of the impact. Unfortunately, there were times when the plane's landing gear collapsed. The resulting crash usually damaged the undercarriage but seldom caused serious injuries. Student pilots with depth perception difficulties usually kept landing and bouncing until they got it right, or they were washed out of flying. That's what happened to Johnny Schmitz, who insisted on landing ten feet above the runway.

I had joined up with a school chum named Doug Smith, and when the time came to leave for Manning Depot, we went as passengers on an overnight CNR train, arriving in Edmonton about 6 a.m. The train had been full of armed forces personnel and civilians by the time it reached Saskatoon, and I think that we stood most of the night. We arrived at the station and were loaded into the back of an RCAF truck for a twenty-minute drive to the exhibition grounds where the barracks were. By the time we were assigned to the various huts that were to be home for the next three weeks, it was lunchtime. We then learned that the general public had been invited to an Armed Forces Day at the exhibition grounds that afternoon, and the entire Manning Depot, about 3,000, was to parade in a March Past. New recruits brought up the rear, and because we were still in our civvies, we got the biggest hand. There weren't enough seats to accommodate all of us, and we were told to line the railing on the inside of the race track. This gave us a terrific view of the proceedings, but as it turned out, we were too close. The first event was a jalopy race, and two of the vehicles locked wheels right in front of us. They went highballing out of control through the fence and knocked about eight guys over like they were tenpins. We often thought how funny it was that their first letter home, after about ten hours in camp, would be from a hospital. The worst injuries were broken arms and legs, one helluva way

Penny Candy, Bobskates

to start your war service.

For the first ten days, we were confined to barracks. We got about six shots the second day in camp, and from then on it was a sixteen-hour day of continual parade-square drilling, starting with wake-up at 6 a.m. The temperature was in the high eighties and low nineties, which really made it tough. The shots were for a whole range of diseases. I was sitting next to a big husky chap who told me that the reason most people faint is because they don't discipline themselves not to think about it. Medics would take each guy into a little room where you couldn't see what was happening, and every once in a while you'd hear a moan and a thud. My husky friend went in before I did, and in a minute or so, I heard a moan and then a thud! The TABT shot was the one that gave the most problems, and the "old hands," guys who had been there two weeks, had all sorts of remedies to prevent your arm from getting stiff. "Swing it around for half an hour, right after the shot" . . . "Have a real hot shower" . . . were a couple. Most of us didn't do anything and only had a minor inconvenience. One of the guys who swung his arm couldn't move it for a week.

We received our entire clothing gear on the second day in camp, including winter gear. I didn't find out until January, when I was stationed in Regina, that my greatcoat was three sizes too big. (My collar buttoned at my navel, which made it somewhat uncomfortable when it was twenty below zero with a twenty mph wind.)

The first thing we did when we got our uniform was to change the shape of the round, solid brass, RCAF insignia, which we wore in our hats. Flat wasn't cool. So we put the insignia face down in the drain of one of the sinks and pounded it with a broom handle to give it a semi-round appearance. That was cool. The objective was to look as much like a veteran as possible. Nobody, but nobody, wanted to look like a raw recruit.

I soon learned to eat a little more quickly than I was used to. At my first meal in the messhall, where about 1,000 sat down at a time, I tried chewing my food ninety times before swallowing (a ritual in our house) and realized I'd probably starve to death by the end of the week. Your meal had to be half-eaten from the tray before you sat down or you'd never have time to finish. I think we had thirty minutes from the time we left the parade square before we had to be back.

and Frozen Roadapples

I also found that inspection in the nude each morning was something I could do without. I didn't stack up too well in my birthday suit beside most of the guys, who looked like they came from muscle beach. We had to parade in front of the Medical Officer, who looked us up and down, and then move back into file. After the second day of this, I decided I didn't like it, so I pulled the age-old routine of hiding in the john. There were about twenty cubicles with about eighteen-inches clearance at the bottom. I would sit on the seat, with my feet off the floor, and each morning the Sergeant would come in, bellow something I never did understand, and then get down on his knees to spot anybody. NCO's, particularly sergeants, had a way of shouting and running their words together so that the whole thing was indistinguishable. You learned to key on the last word. In this particular case, although the shouts were indefinable, his tone left no doubt that he had better not find anybody hiding in the john. And the key word sounded an awful lot like . . . PACKDRILL! I aged. I got away with it for the remaining five days of the "short-arm" inspections.

We had a sobering moment or two on about our fourth day at Manning Depot. We were given a small Bible, issued with our "dogtags" ("wear these around your neck at all times"), and directed to sign our "Last Will and Testament" (something I hadn't spent a lot of time thinking about). The "dogtags" were stamped with your service number (R 218365) and your blood type (O+). One tag was fireproof (that's nice), one was acid proof (a comforting thought . . . ACID? . . . I thought the enemy was firing bullets!), and I don't recall what the third one was for (probably alcohol proof). In my Will I left Mother "all my worldly possessions," which included a couple of pipes, my Rolex watch (which she had given me when I joined up), something less than $100 in my bank account, my old Cub uniform and a pair of skates.

Playing tricks on one another was our way of relieving the boredom of the training period, particularly during the first couple of weeks when we were confined to barracks. The tricks were generally harmless and quite funny from the "trickers" point of view, but not always from the "trickees." I had fallen asleep in my upper bunk just after supper one night, fatigued from drilling all day in the hot sun. I had a nightmare in which I was caught in a torrential rain. I woke up to find myself soaking wet and about fifteen guys enjoying my predicament. One of them had

127

showered me with the ten-gallon stirrup pump intended for firefighting. On another occasion, a very sound sleeper was carried out to the parade square in the middle of the night only to wake up in total bewilderment at the light of dawn as the first units lined up for breakfast.

The double-decker bunks were located side by side, about three feet apart. If you were an upper-bunk occupant, your method of entrance was to use the upper railings of the two bunks like parallel bars and swing yourself into the bunk. You soon learned to check and make sure that all of the springs holding your mattress to the bunk were properly attached. If they weren't, you fell with a thud into the bottom bunk. Your problem was that much greater if the bottom bunk was occupied.

For the most part, tricks were only played on those who could take it as well as dish it out. Those who were having obvious difficulty in adjusting by reason of homesickness, or those who just plain didn't like service life, were left alone. We had one chap who had paid for a hernia operation out of his own pocket in order to pass his medical. Things weren't quite what he had expected, unfortunately, and he was a very unhappy airman. The forty-five men in your flight represented all types of personalities from every social level. The great majority soon learned to accept and even enjoy what Manning Depot had to offer. The few who didn't probably had a miserable time throughout their entire service.

One hot afternoon we were standing on the parade square, about a thousand of us, waiting for some returning war hero to give us a pep talk. Canada's famous fighter pilot, Buzz Beurling, was one of the aces joed into this assignment. It was like a furnace, and although we were "at ease," it got to be real tiresome after close to an hour. I whispered out of the side of my mouth to Doug Smith, "I'll make out I'm going to faint, and you help me to the shade." He whispered back, "You look too red to faint." So I gave up on that one, and the hero finally arrived.

On another day, four of us figured that we had had enough marching in the heat, and we sneaked back to our barracks. These were strictly out-of-bounds during the morning, and you were placed on charge if caught inside. I guess that was to prevent stealing in the barracks. Anyway, four of us were standing around talking when an officer and a sergeant burst through the door, apparently on a regular morning inspection of the huts. We were scared stiff. The sergeant came over to me and hollered, "What are you doing here?'' I couldn't even speak, let alone know what to tell him. He finally bellowed, ''Are you Hut Fatigue?'' to which I mumbled, ''Yes, Sergeant.'' He and the officer then inspected the barracks while we stood like ramrods, and then they left. We later learned that Hut Fatigue are four guys who are joed to make sure the barracks are neat enough to pass inspection. We were really awfully lucky to get out of that one because we probably would have got an additional two hours' drill in the sun.

The drill instructors in Training Wing were corporals who thought they were generals. We thought they were generals, too. They drilled us unmercifully in the hot sun, hour after hour, day after day. They berated us with every derogatory expression imaginable. ''You march like a bunch of pregnant ducks,'' was one of the milder putdowns. They told us that at the end of our training period, we would respond to orders as if we were robots. And they were right. They took a group of misfits, some almost totally uncoordinated, and welded us into a smart, efficient marching unit. They had a tough job, and they did it well. To learn to do close order drills with precision was important, but the most important thing they taught us was discipline. The type of discipline that could save a life under fire.

During the first week, our drill corporal asked for all aircrew who couldn't swim to put up their hands. Without thinking, I put mine up. Our names were then taken, and we were to get up at 5:30 each morning (thirty minutes before reveille) and take swimming instructions at some outdoor pool. When I realized what I had let myself in for, I nearly panicked. I had been afraid of water since my first bath. We were all moved to our own section of the hut so that we wouldn't disturb the others when we got up in the middle of the night. I decided that if I didn't show the first morning, I might get away with it. So I stayed in bed and prayed a lot. Damned if they didn't miss me, and I never had to go. What a stroke of luck.

We had to line up in front of Stores about twice a week to get clean bedding. We had to stuff our dirty sheets in our pillowcases and then exchange them for clean ones. The occasional pillow fight would break out, resulting in torn pillowcases with sheets spewed onto the ground, but the corporal was usually quite tolerant.

Penny Candy, Bobskates

At the completion of the ten days we had been confined to barracks, we were given our first night out. We were all spit and polish and excited about strutting our stuff on "civvy street." On our way out of the hut, our corporal stood beside an enormous cardboard box full of "French safes" and said, "Be sure to take some with you, fellas." *Some*? Not one . . . or two . . .but *some*? What did he think we were, stallions? We each grabbed a handful and thought it was hilarious . . . most of us had never had our very own condom before. But what a waste! . . . (speaking only for myself, of course). Some time around midnight we wound up at a dance in a downtown hall, and after a particularly lively number, I pulled out my handkerchief to wipe my brow. Six condoms rolled onto the dance floor. In a matter of seconds a half-dozen couples were down on their hands and knees. What a lark! And the funny thing was . . . I don't recall being the least bit embarrassed. Such were the times.

Nearly all of the guys would spend each night in the pub, which was on the grounds, but I never went because I was worried about bringing back my kidney condition. As it was, I lost out on a lot of fun. I didn't figure I could go in without drinking, so I would be hanging around outside and hear about thirty verses of the "North Atlantic Squadron." Some nights they would all grab the trolley and go to the airmen's mess at the ITS station across the river. When they returned late at night, they would make the trip somewhat memorable by rocking the trolley going over the "high level" bridge until the more sober were in fear of having to swim back.

I recall that one afternoon we were in downtown Edmonton at a time when draft beer was rationed and the pub could only serve one round an hour. They told me it was so crowded you had to stand and wait for service.

Doug and I finally got our first forty-eight-hour pass, and we caught the train for Saskatoon to show off our uniforms to our friends. It was rushed, but nice to get home.

Towards the end of our training, they asked anyone who would like to take boxing lessons to raise their hands. Three or four of our flight did, and it turned out that they were needed for a services boxing card that night. Apparently they were short a few boxers, and this was their way of filling the card. One of the guys showed up the next morning with a doozy of a shiner, and his nose was a little off centre. Another time when they wanted volunteers, they knew they would have to be cute about it because of the boxing episode. So they asked for anyone who played the piano to put up their hands. Those who did probably thought they would get time off from drill to rehearse for a variety show for the men. It didn't quite turn out that way. They were needed to move a piano from one building to another.

When we were lined up in formation in four ranks of fifteen each, the corporal would give the order to "number from the left." This meant that each man must yell out his number at the top of his lungs in sequence from one to fifteen. If we were feeling particularly foolhardy, the number eleven man would yell "Jack" and the number twelve man, "Queen," and number thirteen, "King." We would be stopped at this point and berated by the corporal, who threatened all sorts of horrible things, and then we would start again. The trick was knowing when to quit this little game. The corporal's patience would gradually exceed its limit, but we knew that he had been one of us not that long ago, and he would be tolerant to a point. When you passed that point, the whole flight was punished, not just the clowns in the front rank. Sometimes we won, sometimes we lost. The important thing that you learned from this was to never be the eleventh man in the front row when lining up because the whole responsibility fell on his shoulders. The problem was that sometimes the guys in the rear rank didn't think it was as funny as you did when you yelled, "Jack!"

After our dental inspection, some chaps had to have their impacted wisdoms out if they were aircrew (because of pressure problems at great heights). One of them lay in his lower bunk with blankets around the side for privacy and groaned for about three days.

At the end of the third week, we had a fairly long exam, with the emphasis on math, and when the results were ready, we had individual interviews with an officer. I was told I was being sent to pre-aircrew training at a school in Winnipeg for two months, attached to No. 3 Wireless Station. This meant that Doug and I would split up because he got posted to ITS (Initial Training School) in Edmonton. Just before we were to be posted, two guys came down with Chicken Pox, and we all thought we would be confined to barracks, which would be total boredom. However, they let us go, and we took the train to Winnipeg, arriving at about 7:30 at night. We were bused to our school and told to try and find a rooming house from the addresses on the blackboard. It was a bit of a lark. We didn't know one street from the other or which ones had already been rented by guys who got to the school ahead of us. Another guy, Johnny Dipple, who looked as bewildered as I did, joined up with me and we started out on foot, lugging two kit bags each full of clothing.

After walking all over hell's half acre, we were flaked out on a boulevard at about 10:30, ready to sleep on our kit bags, when a lad about twelve years of age came over and asked, "Are you fellows looking for a rooming house?" It turned out that he knew of one, and by 11 o'clock we were in our new home. It was a real break because some of the guys had to take a taxi and spend the night in the YMCA and look for rooms after class the next day. Our landlady had two upstairs rooms, each with a double bed, and four of us from the school stayed there. She grew her own vegetables, and the meals were good. Our school, called "Annie Gibson," was only a ten-minute walk. It was in a fairly tough neighbourhood, and we used to joke that the kids going home from kindergarten took turns beating up on the service guys. We had regular school hours and took math, English, and I think one other course, from retired teachers. It was a nice break from being in a station and marching all day.

One Sunday during the latter part of September was designated as a national day of prayer for peace, and we had to leave the rooming house at about 6:30 in the morning to assemble at No. 3 Wireless Station across the city. We wore our winter blues, and I had a cardigan on under my tunic because it was chilly. About 2,500 airmen assembled at the station and the parade wasn't until 1:30, so a chum and I played pool in the mess. We somehow missed the call for lunch and soon found ourselves lining up for the parade. There were approximately 8,000 to 10,000 service personnel in the parade, marching eight abreast. When we passed a large commercial sign giving the temperature, it was seventy-eight degrees. It's the closest I've come to passing out; several did, particularly in the baseball park where we lined up at attention for the prayer service.

Final exams took place the first week in November, and soon after we took a troop train to Regina to ITS. We travelled overnight through

and Frozen Roadapples

ten below zero weather in wooden coaches (vintage 1910) that had absolutely no heat. Light was provided by thin candles hanging from the ceiling, which unwound as they burned. The "newsie" came through our car some time around midnight with his magazines, chocolate bars, sandwiches and oranges. He was selling the oranges at twelve cents each, or three for forty-five cents. We were only half awake, dozing off from time to time on the solid wooden benches, and most of us bought three oranges. We were just too dazed to realize he was conning us.

While I was in Winnipeg, Mother sent me a clipping from the *Star-Phoenix* stating that my chum, Keith Laing, had been killed overseas. I wrote a letter to his mother with great difficulty. What can you say to a widow who has lost her only child to war at twenty years of age? He had been the pilot of a Lancaster bomber which had crashed in England in a bad fog while coming home from a mission. He is buried in Chester, Cheshire, England. A long way from home.

When we arrived in Regina, we were assigned to flights and dormitories. There were forty-three in my flight . . . all new faces, but you soon made friends. An older World War I vet was assigned as our flight leader. He was a nice chap with a fatherly type of attitude. The airforce had taken over the Normal School for the duration, and our dorms were the classrooms. We slept in double bunks in a room with a wall of drafty windows. When it was twenty to thirty below zero, you could see your breath in the room. The upper bunk next to mine was empty, so I used to pull its mattress on top of me for warmth. The guy in the bunk below snored so loudly that if he got to sleep first, most of us would be awake for hours. When he did snore, the bunks on either side took turns throwing Japanese orange peels at his face to make him turn over. You got ten points for a peel in his mouth, five for one that hit the face.

ITS was a no-nonsense school that specialized in math, navigation and armament. When you arrived, you were given the distinctive white flashing for your cap to show that you were aircrew, and when you graduated you were assigned to be either a pilot, navigator, bombardier, wireless airgunner or airgunner. The navigator's position had replaced the early "observer" classification. We had to strip and reassemble the Mark IV Browning machine gun blindfolded. The smallest part, about an inch long, was called the "rear-seal spring retainer keeper and pin."

Penny Candy, Bobskates

(Funny what sticks with you over the years.) My navigation callipers had a bit of a spring to them, which meant that I usually missed the target area by some three hundred miles. The work was hard, and most nights were spent studying. The monotony was usually broken by Saturday night dances on the station. At least once a week, some clown would wake you up around one in the morning to see if you wanted a hamburger. He'd collect orders for at least a half dozen, and then he'd sneak under the fence, walk about two miles, be gone about an hour or more, and wake you up again around 2:30 or 3:00 with a cold hamburger. Really weird.

We had to run around Wascana Lake, a distance of about two-and-a-half miles, once a week in below-zero weather. It was the brainchild of our physical training instructor, who made the run with us. In previous years, some guys had taken a shortcut across the frozen lake, but when one fell in and drowned, they posted NCO's around the lake at checkpoints. I had the same attitude towards this as I did learning to swim. I saw it as a virtually impossible task. The first day we had to make the run, I was out of breath at about the half-mile mark. When the instructor went by me in overdrive, I waited until he was lost in the hoar frost and then did an about-turn and went back. I not only came up to the last checkpoint from the wrong direction, but they didn't even stop to take my name. I figured that with that kind of efficiency, I wouldn't bother even showing up for the next runs. I was never caught. Once again, it wasn't that I was being a smart aleck or that I was copping out. I was just trying to stay within my limitations. In this particular case, we were running in what was virtually gym strip in below-zero weather, and I was trying to avoid getting a bad chill that would take me out of class.

On one forty-eight-hour pass, I went home, and in order to get back in time, I had to take the bus because the train would get me there about three hours too late. When I got on the bus, it was packed, and I had to sit in the aisle on a camp stool. Before the bus pulled out of the station, a bag of apples Mom had given me broke, and a dozen apples rolled all over the aisle. This was the last straw. I hadn't looked forward to an eight-hour trip in an unheated bus anyway. I got off and took the train. Sure enough, the next day I was pulled out of class and charged with being AWOL. I was marched in front of our flight leader in a formal hearing with a mouth so dry I could hardly speak. I explained exactly what happened, and he let me off. That's what I meant when I said he had a fatherly attitude. He probably knew I couldn't run with a rifle over my head for an hour anyway. I was a minor hero for about a day though because I was the only guy in the flight ever placed on charge.

Just before the final exams, I came down with the flu. The "hospital" was a bunch of basement rooms, four to a room. Dirty hot chocolate cups lined the railings. I got a chill the day before when we had marching drill on the parade square. It was about ten below zero with a gusting twenty to twenty-five mph wind. The greatcoat I had been issued at Manning Depot in August (the one that buttoned at my navel) didn't provide any protection, and the wearing of scarves was not permitted. Non-issue scarves were worn off the base, but not on. Our Flight Lieutenant (the "fatherly" one) came over to me when he noticed my secondhand ill-fitting coat and asked the Flight Sergeant to make sure that I was issued with a new coat — "One that fits." I got it the next day, but by then the chill was taking effect. I reported sick around 3:00 in the afternoon and got chewed out for not being on sick parade at 8:00 in the morning. They didn't seem to understand that a person could somehow take ill after sick parade. Anyway, I had a fever, was diagnosed as having the flu and bronchitis and was sent to the base hospital. When I was admitted to my four-bed ward, I could hardly see the room for cigar smoke. Four patients were playing cards in the room. I was told that the next day would be my turn to sweep the ward! Apparently patients were responsible for keeping their own ward clean. After the fifth day of "care," I was anxious to get back to my flight, so I asked to be discharged. I was sitting in the Orderly Room for reassignment when a group of VIPs dropped in, including an Air Vice Marshall, a Group Captain, a Wing Commander and etc. etc. It was the annual surprise inspection that was rather low in the popularity poll. I came to attention, but the Orderly Room Sergeant didn't see them (he was bent over a file cabinet) and was actually threatened with losing his stripes for not coming to attention. It didn't make sense, but that didn't matter.

When I went to my reassigned quarters, I found that my old flight had gone ahead of me, that I was with a new bunch and didn't know a soul. I had a forty-eight-hour pass coming up and went home for the weekend. I wasn't really over the flu, and Mom had the family doctor come to the house. He put me on sulpha drugs, and when I got back on Monday, I had to report on sick leave again.

Many of the service doctors were quite young, twenty-three to twenty-five years of age. That was because the federal government required medical students to complete their seven years' training in five with hardly any time off. They were trying to offset as quickly as possible the number of Canadian doctors who had been lost at Dunkirk. As soon as they graduated, they went into the forces as captains or equivalent rank. Their medicine was straight out of books without the advantage of internship or practice.

When they did a urinalysis, they found the old problem and sent me to a local urologist. The Air Force used him for specialized consulting because he had a son overseas, and he wasn't likely to look too kindly on anyone who was goldbricking. I had to tell him of my history with chronic nephritis and he replied that he was going to recommend me for discharge.

My day of discharge came, and I was given a long form that required about ten different signatures . . . one from the Mess to prove I didn't owe any money . . . one from the Library, that I didn't have any books out . . . one from the Sports Officer, that I didn't have any equipment out (I found him having a shower, and it's the only time I ever saluted an officer who was nude!), and so on. At this point I was glad to be getting out, but I was disappointed that I hadn't made it. I had met some awfully nice guys, and was sure that some of them, even that late in the war, wouldn't make it home.

ITS had been interesting. The test for night vision was conducted in groups of not more than eight and was rather intriguing. After sitting in a semi-dark room for about fifteen minutes with blindfolds over our eyes, we were taken into a totally dark room where the blindfolds were removed. For fifteen minutes, various objects were projected on a screen, which you had to identify. Each person was given a pencil and a pad with raised lines so that you could feel the line with one hand while writing down your answer with the other. In order to prevent you from bending forward to get a closer look at the screen, a chain on the back of each chair was attached to a "dog collar" around your neck. Your night vision capability was graded from the score you made. It was interesting to learn

136

that the best way to view an object at night is to look to one side of it rather than directly at it. Try it some time, and you will find that it works.

Another test we were given was used to determine how well we had learned to identify enemy aircraft. Approximately fifty slides were projected on a screen of aircraft viewed from different angles and at varying distances. You were expected to score at least ninety per cent accuracy.

We also fired handguns on the pistol range. It was to give you some skill with a .38 in case you ever bailed out and were confronted by the enemy. Judging from our scores, I would say that the enemy had little to worry about. Finally, we were required to sit in a room full of tear gas for a couple of minutes without any respirator or eye protection. Some came out of the room with their eyes smarting and welling with tears. Others just pretended. They were the ones smart enough to crouch in a corner where the tear gas, pouring from a canister in the centre of the room, had little effect.

We were also taken in a pressure chamber to about 30,000 feet so that we would recognize the euphoria that comes with the lack of oxygen. I remember that the temperature decreased quite noticeably as the altitude increased. It seems to me that training to be a pilot took about one year from the time you entered Manning Depot, less for other aircrew positions.

It was at ITS where the decision was made as to which member of the aircrew you would be trained for. The decision was based on need and aptitude, with the former getting the priority. In other words, if there was a need to increase the number of pilots due to heavy losses in combat, then a good percentage of ITS graduates would be sent to EFTS (Elementary Flying Training School). The same selection process also applied to the other aircrew positions. However, if your marks indicated that you were better suited to be a navigator, or bombardier, and so on, then that factor would receive serious consideration in your selection.

Upon graduation from your last training school, when your coveted wings were presented by the Commanding Officer during a special ceremony at which your family were invited guests, a good percentage of pilots became commissioned officers. The majority of other aircrew members received their sergeant's stripes. The reasoning behind this apparent discrimination was that pilots were in charge of the aircraft and, therefore, should not be junior in rank to any member of his crew.

Canada's huge expanse and relative safety from direct enemy action made it an ideal site as base for the British Commonwealth Air Training Plan. Its thousands of graduates in both air and ground crews, representing all countries in the Commonwealth, played a major role in the Allies' victory over Germany.

Their Lives Had Barely Begun

It would be inconceivable of me to write a book about my memories as a youth growing up in Saskatoon and not include a chapter to the memory of those friends who sacrificed their lives in the war.

Keith Laing lived on the third floor of the Dorr Block, a walkup apartment across the street from our house in Saskatoon. His father had died when Keith was nine years of age from injuries he suffered when struck down by a cyclist on the sidewalk. All through high school he had a *Star-Phoenix* paper route to help his mother make ends meet. Keith was a talented cartoonist, and in our late teens, we had kicked around the idea of developing a strip for the local paper. He would draw, and I would do the dialogue. In 1942 Keith joined the RCAF and became the pilot of a Lancaster bomber. He was killed when his plane hit a church steeple in a fog while returning from a raid over Germany.

Bud Ross lived two houses down the street. He was big, quiet and on the rough side. But if he liked you, he was a good friend. His uncle had lost all of his fingers down to the second knuckle in a sausage grinder accident in the butcher shop where he worked. We used to watch him exercise with a spring-loaded tension bar pulled across his chest and wonder what would happen if his stubs let go of the grip. Bud, like a number of prairie lads who had never seen an ocean, joined the Navy. He was lost at sea in 1944 when his ship, the *Jervis Bay*, was sunk in a naval engagement.

139

Penny Candy, Bobskates

George Mackie lived in the corner house, across from Keith's apartment block. His dad was a sergeant in the city police for many of the years that we were growing up and later became deputy-chief. We were always a little scared of him and it would add to the excitement when we raided local vegetable gardens or played Halloween pranks. George became a pilot instructor with the RCAF, attached to the RAF at a flying training school in Calgary. He was killed in 1943 when a student pilot froze at the controls.

Bob Grant lived across the back lane on 9th Street, three houses down from ours. One time when we were fighting as kids, I hit him in the face, and his nose bled furiously. Three days later, his parents had a wiener roast for all of the kids on the block but me. I felt terribly left out. Bob became a wireless air gunner (WAG) with the RCAF and was killed in 1944 when his Liberator blew up while on submarine patrol in the Atlantic. Bob and I were friends and neighbours for seventeen years.

Lloyd Tomczak lived on the 300 block of 9th Street with his three brothers and sister. His dad was a music teacher, and you could safely bet that anyone living in Nutana who could play a reed or string instrument had Mr. Tomczak to thank. Lloyd was serving in France with the infantry when he was shot through the head. He was strapped to the wing of a Spitfire and rushed to London for major surgery. The wound left him permanently blind. After the war, he became an executive with the CNIB in Toronto.

Don McEwen lived in a brick house on the corner of Victoria Avenue and 11th Street with his mother, his sister Nora and his father, a family physician. He was husky, athletic, popular and a good student. Don contracted polio while serving in India when he was twenty. He spent the rest of his life in a wheelchair.

Other friends who gave their lives included: Bruce Parker, air navigator; Mickey Tomczak, bomber pilot; Jack O'Grady, pilot; Bernard Wilkinson, air gunner; Mert Zaphe, air gunner; and Jim Smith, pilot. They were all school chums and among the many graduates of Nutana Collegiate who were killed in action during the war.

I often think about them and ask myself: What would they be like today? What would they have achieved in life? And then I think about what I have been privileged to do: married for thirty-nine years, three

and Frozen Roadapples

wonderful children, four beautiful grandchildren, retired for ten years and travelled extensively. That is when the magnitude of their sacrifice hits home. Most of those lads were twenty years of age, the oldest was twenty-three. They were shot from the skies, drowned in the world's oceans and killed on foreign battlefields. Some are buried in countries thousands of miles from home. Others were never found. Many who returned had permanent physical impairments, and others had deep-seated psychological scars that would haunt them to an early grave. Their lives had barely begun. What a terrible, terrible waste.

May their souls rest in peace. May they be remembered always. Today's young men and women must never forget the sacrifices made by their peers of yesteryear, and above all, they must ensure that such sacrifices never become necessary again.

In 1940 the Liberal government under Prime Minister McKenzie King passed the National Resources Mobilization Act, which conscripted men for home defence, but not for overseas service. By 1942, of the approximately 157,000 men who had been conscripted, 87,000 had volunteered for active duty overseas. Home defence camps were set up in British Columbia, on the prairies and in Quebec.

In 1942, after Japan had entered the war, the King government called a plebiscite, seeking approval to send conscripted men overseas where replacements were desperately needed. English-speaking Canada voted approval overwhelmingly, but Quebec voted three to one against the measure. King was too astute a politician to offend Quebec, and it wasn't until late in the war that he consented to sending conscriptees overseas.

Exemptions from service were granted to war plant employees, whose work was vital to the war effort, and to farmers because, as the old saying goes, "an army marches on its stomach." Exemptions were also given to the physically unfit (4F), and to university students, with the provision that they had to maintain at least a sixty-five per cent average. The federal government, through its National Selective Service, made it illegal for employers to hire single, male Canadians in a variety of occupations, from the entertainment industry to selling used cars. And what about those high school friends who went to university for four years while the great majority went to war? As far as I am aware, no one bore them any malice. Volunteering to join up was a purely personal decision. Some joined because of peer pressure, others because of a sense of adventure, and some because of an older brother in the service, or a father who was a World War I veteran. A few were drafted, and some (mostly older chaps) enlisted through a sense of patriotism, or they had been out of work so long, they were glad to get something to do. Those who went on to university were graduating when their friends (not all) were returning from war. Their advantages were obvious. What they missed was a once-in-a-lifetime experience, and they would never know the special friendship shared by comrades-in-arms.

Memorial avenues of trees, memorial cenotaphs, memorial arenas, all are fitting remembrances to the 42,000 Canadians killed in World War II. But they are subject to the ravages of time, progress and circumstance . . . Trees may become blighted, arenas old and unsafe, cenotaphs may have to be relocated. It is the permanency of the remembrance, etched in the hearts and minds of succeeding generations, that is the most important memorial of all.

"This is the Canadian Broadcorping Castration"

Following my discharge from the RCAF in January, 1944, I started my less than spectacular but extremely interesting career in radio. I happened to see a classified ad in the *Star-Phoenix* for an announcer at CFQC. Radio broadcasting had been an interest of mine from the time, some years before, when I used to listen to a local announcer by the name of Clyde Harrington do a late-night program called "Coals From Off The Altar." It sounded like a great way to make a living. Following an interview by Vern Dallin, I was auditioned by Wilf Gilby, a well-known CFQC personality for many years, and was hired. Probably the most prominent alumnus of CFQC is "Cactus" Jack Wells, who started as a sportscaster back in the '30s, and whose son Jack has followed in his father's footsteps with TSN. By the time I had made my appearance, CFQC had been around a long time. A.A. Murphy put the station on the air on July 18, 1923, with its first broadcast from their studios at 1323 Osler Street.

As I was to find there and at three subsequent stations, being an announcer was fun, demanding and somewhat exhausting. We worked long hours for what was minimum wage and could be replaced at a moment's notice by an aspiring novice who felt that the "glamour" of a radio career made up for the lack of pay. Remember now, I'm speaking of more than forty years ago. Staff turnover was so high that after three

Penny Candy, Bobskates

months at CFQC, I was senior announcer, which says something for the quality of our work. When broadcasters can't get their tongues to behave and letters become transposed, you come up with what the industry calls a "spoonerism." The word is supposed to have originated many years ago with a Rev. Spooner, who one Sunday morning observed from the pulpit, "I notice some of you are occupewing the wrong py."

I did a lot better than that on several occasions. We were trying so hard on the commercials of one particularly important account, that none of us could do it right, and Wilf Gilby had to come in off-duty to read them. The account was Bapco Paint, and the phrase that gave us difficulty was "Bapco Porch Floor Paint." No matter how hard we tried, the words came out either "Blapco," or "plorch," or "plaint," or any combination thereof, and sometimes all three. Which the sponsor didn't find to be terribly amusing.

Another local announcement that gave our brilliant staff some difficulty was, "Belgian Drycleaners — Dyers and Furriers"; we could never seem to get it right. We insisted on saying, "Belgium." An example of major spoonerisms made into one announcement would go something like this: "Ladies and gentlemen, for the past thirty minutes you've been listening to the famous Mormon Tablenacker Choir. The program has been brought to you by McGavin's Bread. Remember, for the breast in bed, it's McGavin's. This is the Canadian Broadcorping Castoration. Now stay tuned for an address by Sir Stifford Crapps!!" A classic spoonerism on American radio came out this way and was heard by a nationwide audience: "Ladies and gentlemen, from the White House in the nation's capitol, the President of the United States, Mr. Hoobert Hever." CFQC listeners were a little startled one day when they heard the following announcement: "Attention local squirrels. Be sure to stock your shelves with famous Grocer Brand peanut butter."

The excitable sportscaster was an accident waiting to happen. Like the Regina broadcaster in the '40s who gave the following play-by-play in the heat of a sudden-death overtime period: "Ferguson stick handles down the boards . . . He's at centre ice . . . He crosses the blueline . . . He takes a shit on goal. HE SCORES!" Some listeners phoned to protest the language; others to enquire about the goalie.

Three afternoons a week CFQC broadcast the names and conditions of patients from rural areas. They would be listed as "Serious," "Fair," or

and Frozen Roadapples

"Good," and quite often the family would be advised that the patient "Can be taken home tomorrow." The introduction to the program went something like this: "For the convenience of family and friends who find it difficult to travel to Saskatoon, we are pleased to bring you the names and conditions of patients from outlying areas, in both St. Paul's and city hospitals." We had an announcer on staff who was absolutely hopeless without a script. His lack of ability to ad lib was matched by his tendency to mumble. Seconds before he was to do the program one afternoon, we confiscated the script from the studio. His ad lib, preceded by frantic arm-waving and a look of total panic, went along these lines: "I'M ON?? . . . (pause) . . . Oh . . . hello. We have a list . . . if you live on a farm . . . these are patients in Saskatoon . . . some are pretty sick." Improved roads, increased telephone services and the building of several small hospitals eliminated the need for such a program by the early 1950's.

The fun part of radio usually took place during the night shift when no one from management was around. At CFQC we used to place orange peels on the turntables, increase the speed from 33 1/3 to 78 rpm's and then push the "stop" button. The winner was the one whose peel went the farthest distance. Stan Clifton, the station's engineer, who was with A.A. Murphy from the beginning, could never understand how orange peels got into the control panel. Horsing around served its purpose in radio. It helped to relieve the tension that is part of broadcasting. Nothing could match the fun of getting someone to laugh when they were in the middle of an announcement. The time for your best shot was to wait for a fifteen-minute newscast, the only time an announcer had to keep going to the bitter end. There was no way that you could play a musical selection in order to get time to recover your composure during a newscast. So it was during the nightly news that some of the weirdest things took place. It takes tremendous self-control not to break up when someone is standing immediately in front of you with a vacuum hose sticking out of his pants and wearing a toilet seat around his neck!

One of the most difficult pranks to endure is to sit in a studio, calmly reading the news, while someone proceeds to undress you. I avoided total nudity by hooking my feet around the legs of the chair and holding on for dear life. It's practically impossible to keep some of the incidents from management, who monitor the station every minute it is on the air. During one of my newscasts at CKRM, I noticed the door of the studio

Penny Candy, Bobskates

open as a hand shoved in a smouldering wastebasket. Two or three minutes later, I erupted into spasms of coughing.

I worked at CFQC for five months and then decided to enrol in a commercial course at the Technical Collegiate. Following the course's completion in May, 1945, I was hired by CKRM in Regina, where I worked for a year. Staff announcers at that time included the Hill brothers from Saskatoon, Tom, Jack and Bob, and a chap who was to become quite prominent in CBC-TV, Toronto, Bill Walker. It is probably the only time in the history of Canadian radio that three brothers were announcers on the one station at the same time.

My first problem took place on my third day at the station when I became confused between the cough switch and the control room buzzer. I thought I had cut myself off the air as I frantically rummaged through a pile of papers for a commercial that was due, all the time cussing the stupid commercial for getting misplaced. Unfortunately, the listeners were getting every word loud and clear while the operator was getting a headache from the continuous buzzing in the control room.

I had the morning shift at the station, which required me to sign on at 6: 45 a.m. and work through until 4:30 in the afternoon. I was all alone until 8:00 each morning, but the first quarter hour featured Alberta Slim live, and that gave me time to organize my records and the news. I don't remember much about Slim except that he was a little guy with a statuesque blonde wife whose legs were about six feet long. His repertoire was somewhat limited at the time, and his favourite song was "Don't Shoot the Bartender — He's Half Shot Now." He told me that he didn't really care what people thought (obviously) because he was "laughing all the way to the bank." He later toured Canada with his horse "Kitten," which was, according to Slim, the best trained horse in the country. Apparently it could sleep standing up.

The amount of time that I had to prepare a fifteen-minute newscast depended upon the length of a long-playing recording, usually just over three minutes. I would run back to the newsroom and grab a roll of several feet of news from the Associated Press teletype. During the newscast, the roll was placed on the floor, and the news was read as I reeled it up between my legs. This usually worked out alright until you came to two or three rows of nothing but numbers, the result, I was told,

and Frozen Roadapples

of atmospheric interference on the transmission lines. It called for some pretty fancy ad libbing, particularly if the breakdown was in the middle of extracts from a speech by someone like Churchill or Roosevelt.

At CKRM some of us started our own "Happy Gang," a take-off from the extremely popular CBC program which featured Bert Pearl as emcee. Shirley (our receptionist) played piano; Sid Jacklin (announcer) played the tenor saxophone; Jack Hill (production) and Bob Hill (announcer) both sang; someone played the guitar, and I emceed. We rehearsed on our own time and were on the air for thirty minutes, twice a week, for about two months. The program was popular, but it was just too much to expect staff, who were already working their butts off, to do so much overtime. It was fun while it lasted.

The single music format, that is to say, one type of music broadcast exclusively, was not used as extensively forty years ago as it is today. Competition in today's marketplace compels commercial radio to select a format they hope will be successful in keeping their ratings competitive. They will be known as a "rock" station, "country," "easy listening" and so on. In my morning show at CKRM, I appealed to all musical tastes by playing in each quarter hour a western selection, a pop music number, a military march and an instrumental.

On one typical forty-below morning, I was half asleep at the control panel when I turned around and almost had a cardiac arrest. I thought a grizzly bear had somehow found its way into the station. It turned out to be a six-foot-six member of the local constabulary, wearing a full-length buffalo coat. For the next couple of weeks, he dropped in most mornings, and we would chat on the air. His visits suddenly stopped, and I didn't see him for about a month until I bumped into him on a downtown street. "Where have you been?" says I. "You damn near got me fired," says he. "How?" says I. "The Chief heard you talking to me one morning when I was supposed to be checking the warehouse district!"

In our newsroom at CKRM we had the teletype news services of the Associated Press and the British United Press. Both machines were going for most of the day, transmitting news stories, weather reports, sports scores, special features and so on. Major news stories were, of course, about the war, which was, by the spring of 1945, winding down. It was just a matter of time before the Germans would capitulate. Extremely important news flashes, or bulletins, were preceded by five short clangs of the teletype bell. Most newsrooms were not manned all day, and the bell told everyone within earshot that a major news story was breaking. It was quite a game among the announcing staff to see who could come up with the biggest bulletin. Chuck Cook (Conservative MP) was on staff in 1945 and was lucky enough to be on duty when the bulletin announcing Roosevelt's death was received. But we were all waiting for "The Big One," as we called it, the bulletin announcing armistice. By good fortune, I was alone on duty when the teletype bell went mad. I dashed into the newsroom, ripped the item from the machine, interrupted the musical selection being broadcast, read the bulletin, repeated it and then went into the format we had developed for the announcement of peace in Europe, which was to play the national anthems of each allied power. The boss, Bill Speer, phoned from his home with some concern: "Are you sure that you're right? I haven't heard a word about the armistice on any other station, including the CBC!" I assured him that the news was authoritative, and it turned out that we scooped the other local station, CKCK, by three minutes, and the CBC by about five. The problem for the CBC staff would be that they would have to clear the bulletin through channels before broadcasting, whereas I was able to get it on the air immediately. I still have that BUP news bulletin in my scrapbook. It was quite an exciting and somewhat emotional moment for a young announcer alone on duty that morning of May 8, 1945.

I was often kidded about how I made my living. "You sit at a table and read . . . what a soft touch!" Little did they know. Many times when you were broadcasting, you were also operating the control console. This was particularly true when you were alone on shift. The control panel had eight knobs and several switches, as well as a V.I. Indicator (volume control). This equipment operated the four turntables and the studio microphones. It was not unusual to sit at the console, wearing earphones for a CBC timecheck, with the four turntables ready to go . . . one with the program's theme, the second and third with commercial transcriptions and the fourth with a musical selection cued up. At the same time that you were listening to the CBC, you were also signing off the program, bringing up the theme music, fading the theme and running the commercial. There was also the daily broadcast log on the console where the time of each program and commercial had to be noted and initialed. All this, plus answering the phone because you were also the station receptionist until 9:00 in the morning and after 5:00 at night. And you did this five days a week, ten hours a day. Soft touch be damned.

One morning on our "Happy Gang" program Bill Walker and I sang a number that was popular in the days of vaudeville, "Gallagher and Sheehan." The lyrics were a little tricky and at our rehersal Bill was perfect, but I couldn't get the timing right. Bill coached me through a half dozen runs, but I was always off. Then came the morning of the program . . . I got it bang on. And Bill got it wrong! I don't think he ever forgave me for that.

After a year at CKRM, including a winter of walking through snowdrifts at 6 in the morning, I decided to throw in the towel. One of the problems was my boarding house, which held parties at least once a week. The parties, together with my ten-hour shifts, were taking their toll. It was hard to ignore the former, and difficult to sustain both, so I quit. As if I didn't have enough on my platter, Bill Walker had talked me into taking a principal role in the "Desert Song," being performed by the Regina Operatic Society and directed by Bill Reid. The three months of rehearsals, combined with the one week of performance (with no time off from work), had been a little much. Bill got the lead dancer (he and Marilyn would marry within the year), and I got the flu.

In all honesty, I had been a popular "morning man" and, locally, was a bit of a big fish in a small pond. Among other things, I had started "The Society For the Preservation of Jerks," and the station was in the process of getting lapel buttons made that said "I Am A Jerk." In order to qualify for a button, the listener had to send me three jokes that were suitable for broadcasting. The idea really took off. When I left CKRM, the promotion manager for Simpson's had been planning to put a paper mache model of me in a store window, surrounded by recordings, in a mockup of a control room. I would have liked to have seen that.

I enrolled in the College of Commerce at the university, sponsored by my DVA grants. The college was housed in the former barracks of the RCAF at the airport, and I went to classes as a passenger on Tommy Cameron's Harley Davidson motorcycle. That also had its exciting moments. Like the time we went out of control, narrowly missed a bicyclist, went up the curb and down the sidewalk, losing my heel in the process. When I looked back, the chap was walking his bicycle.

I am not too sure that I was cut out to be at university as a student. I peaked at Christmas with honours in calculus, but after that, it was downhill all the way. Instead of reading the entire "Romeo and Juliet" for an English literature assignment, I went to the movie of the same name, playing at the Capitol. I learned the hard way that Hollywood took considerable license with major works, including Shakespeare's. When my English professor told me that I had written the worst paper in his twelve years on the faculty, I decided that a career in radio may not be too bad after all. The truth of the matter is that I would have liked to continue my university studies, but by this time, I had been living alone with Mother for something like seven years, and it was time to leave. We got along remarkably well, but I felt that it was better for both of us to head out on my own.

Yearning for warmer climates, I made plans to head for British Columbia. It was at this point that fate intervened in the person of Jack Hall. Jack's distinguished father, Emmett Hall, was later to become Canada's Chief Justice, but his influence on my life at that point in time took the form of a twelve-cylinder Lincoln. Jack was motoring to Banff, and he convinced me that by sharing the gas and oil in his father's car, I could save considerable money on my original plan to travel by train. What we didn't know was that the car had a voracious appetite for oil. Eventually we had to load the trunk with quarts of oil, and we had the distinct impression that we could actually look back on those straight stretches of prairie highway and see the last spot we had added oil. That car cost me exactly $3.24 more than if I had taken the train.

In Banff I learned of an opportunity to work at CFJC in Kamloops and decided to apply for the job. It was a bad decision. CFJC's entire staff consisted of two announcers, a receptionist/writer, a transmitter engineer, a production manager, a sales manager and the station's owner, Ian Clark. It was a bare-bones operation. I worked from 7 a.m. to 3 p.m., and John Sharp worked the night shift of 3 p.m. to midnight. If you were sick, you worked. If you were almost dead, you worked. On a hot day, the temperature in the control room would be 115 degrees. One day John and I both got a bug which necessitated several rushed trips to the washroom.

and Frozen Roadapples

The only long-play recording the station had was "The Rhapsody in Blue," which lasted three minutes and forty-two seconds. It was a lifesaver. John and I played the record a total of twelve times that day, and I suspect that some Kamloops residents thought we were celebrating George Gershwin's birthday.

John and I volunteered to improve the file system in the record library (it's amazing what you'll do when you are young and full of drive!). The 78's were in disarray, and it was extremely difficult to find a recording you needed in a hurry, particularly requests from listeners. We worked long and hard to get the several hundred records in alphabetical order. On the day that we finished, we marched into the boss's office and declared the project completed and successful. "That's excellent fellows. Get me my favourite recording . . . Mart Kenny's, 'The West, A Nest, and You'. We have two copies of it. I'll time you." It should have taken less than a minute. Twenty minutes later we admitted defeat. When I left the station weeks later, we still hadn't found them. It was depressing.

I decided to leave CFJC shortly before Christmas, 1947. I had promised to fill in for John so he and his wife could go to the movies, but the day had been a little much. I had been given a shot of penicillin for a strep throat and should have been home in bed. In my fuzzy frame of mind, I fouled up a popular half-hour program called, "The Green Hornet," by playing the last half first. It confused a number of listeners, whose wrath was exceeded by that of the production manager. He hastened my decision to leave, which was influenced, to a great extent, by the opportunity to spend Christmas at home. My next move took me to Victoria. It turned out to be the best move I ever made.

In 1948 CJVI's studios were located on the top floor of the Central Building, a seven-storey office building in downtown Victoria. And this presented a problem. With the building's elevator operator off duty on the weekend, it meant that we had to climb twelve flights of stairs to get to work. If your shift included Saturday night sign-off at midnight and Sunday morning sign-on at seven, it was not uncommon, particularly during spells of bad weather, to sleep on the sofa in the boss's office. This presented a real dilemma to one of the announcers, Laurie Dillabaugh, on a miserable Saturday evening in January. Prior to bedding down on the sofa, he proceeded out of the office, through the reception area and out of the station entrance to the bathroom in the hall. To his dismay, he found the station door locked on his return trip. There was a sense of panic as he took stock of his situation. He was locked out at one in the morning on the seventh floor of an empty office building in winter, wearing jockey shorts and nothing else.

After pondering his fate and his alternatives, he decided on the only plausible course of action open to him. He walked down the twelve flights of stairs, went out of the building entrance onto the street, proceeded around the corner and down the back alley, jumped up to catch the bottom run of the fire escape, hauled himself up and climbed seven storeys to the station. He forced the window of the record library and finally bedded down on the sofa, a little worse for the wear and much the wiser. Next time he would make damned sure that the lock wasn't set on the station door! Laurie was grateful for one thing. No one, particularly the police, had seen him parading around town in his jockey shorts!

It was at a CJVI staff party that I witnessed a fascinating demonstration of mind control. Shortly after midnight, the party had reached the point where things were starting to drag and people were talking about going home. Fred Usher, salesman and founder of the popular Western music group, "The Hometowners," offered to demonstrate what a number of minds concentrating on the same thing could accomplish. He made the point that everyone had to cooperate, "otherwise it won't work."

Here is how he explained what we were going to attempt with the approximately thirty people in attendance. "I am going to ask for a volunteer to leave the studio, and in their absence we are going to decide on one action-word, like 'shout,' 'crawl,' 'sing,' 'whistle,' and so on, that we will try to get the volunteer to do, through the power of concentration. We will form a large circle, holding hands, with the volunteer in the centre." He concluded with the warning that, "if anyone laughs or otherwise breaks the spell, it won't work." Although we were all highly sceptical, we agreed to give it a fair trial, and Al Collins (an announcer) was our first volunteer. When he left the room, we agreed to concentrate on the word "sing."

The lights were partly dimmed, we formed a circle, Al stood in the middle with his eyes shut, we all held hands, and we concentrated. After close to a minute of total silence, Al started to sway slightly and, in a halting voice, started to sing: "Oh . . . Danny boy . . . the pipes . . . the pipes . . . are . . . calling." Someone gasped, the spell was broken, and Al looked like he was coming out of an hypnotic trance. It was really weird. By this time we had a roomful of believers.

Ida Bianco (copy writer) was the next to volunteer, and we thought we would try to cross her up by choosing the same action-word, "sing." After slightly more than a minute of standing in the middle of the circle, she started to talk and spell out, in a hesitating manner, the word "sing." Fred explained that, from what he understood about mind control, she had demonstrated a strong will by not giving in to our demands to sing, but rather, she chose to spell it out.

The third volunteer was Al McMillan, station accountant. We decided to use the word "crawl." Al was a big, husky chap who had specialized in Greco-Roman wrestling while attending UBC. To see him get down on his hands and knees and start to crawl around the studio was mind boggling. He told us that when Fred slapped his face to bring him out of it, "it was like a red hot needle being stuck into my head." It wasn't until the next day that we learned the whole damned thing had been prearranged! What a letdown.

Forty years ago the broadcasting industry was much less sophisticated than it is today. In some ways, the differences defy comparison. Microphones were large and cumbersome; most recorded commercials were on a glass-based disc that broke if you looked sideways at it; remote broadcasts were a gamble as to quality and reliability; and musical selections were played at 78, 45 or 33 rpm's, on one of four control panel turntables. Tape cassettes and the electronic wizardry incorporated in today's control room were several years in the future. It was, therefore, with considerable excitement that CJVI received its first portable wire recorder in 1949. It was a new toy for the announcing staff. We used to sing (every announcer thinks he can sing), tell jokes and record announcements on the wire, and then marvel at the fact there was immediate playback. This frivolous use of the industry's newest invention led to a most embarrassing incident.

One Saturday night after sign-off, two of us located the wire recorder in the sales office and proceeded to record several ribald songs learned during our stint in the RCAF. Our big mistake was that we neglected to erase the wire before returning it to the sales office. We had no idea that a special program had been recorded on the wire for presentation Monday morning to a prominent businessman, a potential sponsor. You can imagine how the station manager and sales staff felt at this audition for VIPs when "The North Atlantic Squadron," sung off-key but with considerable enthusiasm, came blaring out of the recorder.

And then there was the announcer who rushed into the control room one winter's morning at the start of his 11 o'clock shift. He knew that the 11 a.m. program was a CBC origination from Ottawa, and when he didn't hear any sound, he panicked. "Dead air," or silence, is the bane of an announcer's existence. It is usually the result of transmission difficulties and may last anywhere from a few seconds to a major breakdown. He grabbed the only recording available and slipped it onto the turntable. That is why Victoria was shocked to hear "She'll Be Coming Around The Mountain When She Comes" in the middle of the November 11th Remembrance Day one minute of silence!

I knew exactly how he felt. One Christmas Eve I cut the final "hallelujah" off the Hallelujah Chorus from the Messiah. I had been distracted momentarily while I cut off the sound to cue up a commercial recording. I cut back in during the pause before the final, resounding, "HALL-EHH-LOOO-YAH." I thought that the music was concluded and signed off the program. Neither the sponsor nor several music lovers were amused. There are seven "hallelujahs" in the final chorus, so I always responded to any kidding from the staff with the comment, "Well, six out of seven ain't bad."

In 1949 I received the first talent fee that CJVI paid to a staff announcer. Here is how that historical event took place: Salesman Ralph Pashley sold the 11:00 to midnight Saturday Night Dance Party to Brock Whitney, jeweller. Brock agreed to sponsor the program provided that "Bob Thompson is the emcee." Now, my Saturday evening shift ended at 11 p.m., and so Ralph persuaded the station manager, M.V. Chestnut, to pay me a talent fee for that extra hour. The amount agreed upon by all three parties (including me!) was seventy-five cents a program. Those were the good old days of radio!

The staff Christmas party in 1950 almost marked my premature demise from the station. It was traditional in most radio stations that one or two staff members would volunteer to write a play for presentation to the staff, their spouses, and invited guests (usually prominent sponsors). Staff members would take various roles in sketches that contained humorous and satirical references to certain employees and events of the past year. Our play was followed by a quartet, in which I sang tenor, singing lyrics of the Don Rickles put-down type of humour. And that was where my trouble began. One of the lines was quite critical of the boss. At the last minute, the other members of the quartet had decided to delete the line because they thought it may prove to be offensive, particularly with prominent local businessmen in attendance. They never got around to telling me. I was the only one who sang the questionable lyrics, which everyone thought were hilarious, including the boss's wife. But not the boss. They told me afterwards that he was the only one in the whole room who wasn't laughing. Our relationship was somewhat cool for months following the party.

Speaking of Christmas, time has been kind to the prominent politician who, one Christmas Eve many years ago on a national broadcast on the CBC said, "And now, I would like to conclude by wishing every Canadian, from the shores of Newfoundland to the coast of British Columbia, a Very Chrappy Histmas!" Who can remember his name? But, of course, that kind of thing happens to everyone at one time or another. Just last week in the fish and chip shop I ordered "two chips and three pisses of feesh."

At CKRM I had a program called, "What Do You Know, Joe?" which was introduced by the Andrew Sisters singing a chorus from their recording of the same name. Each show featured three telephone calls with cash prizes. Three calls, three different questions, three mornings a week. I was responsible for coming up with the questions, and after a few months, it became a bit of a problem. One day, more or less out of frustration, I asked, "What was the colour of Napoleon's white horse?" After the program signed off, we had two telephone calls asking for the answer!

Forty years ago the give-away programs, for cash or merchandise, were conducted in a rather "unusual" way. I am quite sure that things are different today. To illustrate what I mean, let us take a "mailbag" format as an example. Listeners were told to mail in their answer to a sponsor's question, along with a proof of purchase, and each week the announcer would "dip into the old mailbag" to see if the entry which was drawn was a winner. What he did, in fact, was to make sure ahead of time that the letter he drew did not have the correct answer. The reason was simple enough. The "jackpot" increased each week that the prize was not won, and it was to the advantage of both the program and the sponsor to have the prize grow to a sizeable figure. This guaranteed the station an increasing audience and continued sponsorship.

CBC radio did the same thing, and I was always a little surprised that listeners didn't think it strange that one week the letter drawn from the mailbag would be from British Columbia, the next from Ontario, the third week from Alberta and the fourth from Newfoundland. That wasn't by coincidence, it was by design. The production staff was doing this to give the program widespread appeal, and they couldn't gamble on drawing six letters over a six-week period from just one, or maybe two, provinces.

We did the same thing with programs that featured telephone calls, supposedly picked at random from the directory. We would make sure that we jumped from surnames beginning with "B" to "W" to "D" and back to "M" so that it looked fair to everybody. The one thing we never did was to phone a friend or pick a friend's letter. That would have been, at the least, unethical. What we actually did was considered "good programming."

In the 1940's it was common practise for announcers to hold their script in the right hand and cup the left hand over their left ear. This is what actors like Jack Carson did in the movies when they played the role of a broadcaster, and of course, we copied their style. Actually, there was another reason for that particular mannerism. Early in our broadcasting career, we learned that we do not hear ourselves as others hear us. The reason for this is that our voice is projected forwards, towards those in front of us, and split seconds later, it returns and is picked up by our own ears. By cupping a hand over an ear, we improved our hearing and, therefore, got a more accurate impression of the tonal qualities of our voice. With improved microphones and sophisticated transmitting equipment, announcers no longer have to portray their movie stereotypes.

I worked at CJVI for four years but started to become disenchanted with radio. From observing the moves of various friends in the industry, it was apparent that broadcasting was a transient way of life. Married, and with one child by this time, I wanted to establish some roots. I opted

and Frozen Roadapples

to become a public servant and joined the provincial government where I was employed for the next twenty-eight years.

Radio had been a most interesting, somewhat unusual, and rather exciting way to make a living. But it had been terribly frustrating. You see, after seven years' experience in four different stations, I had never been able to surpass the record I set for distance in the orange peel event at the "Turntable Olympics" at CFQC back in 1944.

Sage Advice from a Wise Old Man

I remember when I was quite young that my grandmother was very ill with an arthritic condition which was in almost every joint in her body. It would be around 1931. I used to go with Mother on her regular visits to their home, but when her condition got so bad that she used to cry out in pain for hours on end, Mother stopped taking me with her. My grandmother was ill for several months, and none of the medications or treatments of the day seemed to help. Finally, more or less in desperation, her doctor said that he had read about a new heat lamp (presumably ultraviolet) that was available in England and was reputed to be very effective in cases of severe arthritis. My grandfather immediately ordered one from the British manufacturer. It took almost two months for the lamp to arrive, and treatment began the moment it was unpacked. My grandmother was completely cured within two weeks and showed no signs of arthritis when she died fifteen years later at the age of eighty-four. It seemed like a miracle, and her recovery was the talk of the local medical fraternity.

My grandfather became quite ill in 1940. I am not too clear on the nature of his illness, except that I know that he had to get his gall bladder removed and, following that, he had some complications. He was in a private ward in the City Hospital for over three months, and when he came home, I recall my mother and my Aunt Olive discussing a statement they had been given by the hospital for $2,120 (including private nursing services). The hospital had said that they would reduce the bill by the $120, providing the full amount was paid immediately. Socialized medicine in Saskatchewan was still seven years down the pike!

Grandpa was confined to his bed, and my mother and aunt, his only surviving family, took turns sitting in the hall by the bedroom door to take care of his needs. His days were obviously numbered, and this ritual continued until he passed away. Towards the end he had brief periods of rationality and then would lapse into a deep sleep. His nourishment was mostly ginger ale. One afternoon, when I was visiting in the hallway with my aunt, Grandpa recognized my voice and called for me. I had been very close to my grandfather, who was a surrogate dad, and I was the only grandchild in the city at the time of his illness. When he called my name, I looked at my aunt to see what I ought to do, and she said, "Wait here, dear, and I'll see what Father wants." She came out in a matter of seconds and said, "He says he wants to give you some advice."

I was a little startled when the importance of what was about to transpire crossed my fertile mind. Here was this wise, old man who had left home with nothing at the age of nineteen, who came West and made a small fortune, who was now going to pass on to his teenaged grandson some sage advice that may very well make me a wealthy businessman in the years to come. I went into his bedroom, stood at the foot of the bed and said, "How are you doing, Grandpa?" He opened his eyes, stared at me and whispered, "Come here, Bobby." I went to the head of the bed, bent forward to speak into his ear and said, "You wanted to give me some advice, Grandpa?" A minute or so passed, and I thought maybe he had gone to sleep. Then he opened his eyes with a start, looked me full in the face and said, just as clear as a bell, "Never shoe a wet horse!" The effort had been too much and he fell into a deep sleep.

When I came out of the room, my aunt looked at me with great expectation and said in a constrained voice, "What did he say?" My aunt was obviously determined that any advice I had received was going to be considered part of the estate, and her two sons were going to share it.

"He said, 'Never shoe a wet horse.'"

She was incredulous. "He said WHAT?"

I repeated, "Never shoe a wet horse."

Penny Candy, Bobskates

"SHOW?" she exclaimed.

"SHOE," I replied.

With a "don't you con your old aunty" look, she asked, "Why wet?"

"I don't know, Aunty, that's all he said."

She looked through me, gave a quick glance into the room, and stomped off down the hall. To her dying day I am not too sure that she ever believed me.

Over the years I have agonized many hours trying to figure out what on earth my grandfather meant. As each of my three children reached a certain age, I took them to one side and passed on his advice. The whole family now knows that you never shoe a wet horse. Unfortunately, it doesn't mean a damn thing.

From what my friends tell me I'm beginning to think that old men make up baffling "pearls of wisdom" to hand down out of a distorted sense of humour. Here are a couple of gems, followed by my interpretation. According to Gordon Butler, his grandfather said, "A wet bird never flies at night." (It's dangerous to go out in the dark in the rain.) Chuck McLeod's elderly uncle left this gem: "It's a sad town where there aren't any strangers." (In most small towns, everyone knows everyone else's business.) I think I'll leave my grandchildren with something like: "Never play a game where the game plays you." Let them toss at night trying to figure that one out!

Tying the Knot, and So On

Doris Dillabaugh and I were married in Victoria on January 6, 1951. We had first met through her brother, Laurie, when he and I were announcers at CKRM in Regina back in 1946. She was only eighteen at the time, fresh out of high school, and I was twenty-three. An evening at the movies was the extent of our relationship. However, when she visited Laurie in Victoria in the summer of 1950, she had matured into an attractive young lady, and the spark was rekindled.

Doris had been encouraged by her brother to give broadcasting a try, and soon after high school graduation, she landed one of the few plums that radio had to offer. She became known as "Mary Hamilton," the radio voice for Simpson's Department Store. She was responsible for four fifteen-minute programs each day of the week, two on CKRM and two on CKCK. She had to write, produce and announce each program. It was a big job for a relatively young girl. "Mary Hamilton" became well-known throughout southern Saskatchewan for the next two years. When the store cut back on its advertising budget in 1950, the programs were cancelled, and it was at that point that Doris decided to visit Victoria. Her "visit" became permanent when CJVI offered her a job. She was to become the first female disc jockey in Victoria, and quite possibly the entire province, with her late-night program, "Dillabaugh Delivers," which began in the winter of 1950.

Prior to our marriage, I had been living with Ted and Irene Reynolds (CBC-TV sports) in their home in Esquimalt, and travelled around town in a 1929 Buick that I had purchased from "Smiling Ben," the used car dealer. Buying that car was quite an experience. A friend told me about

161

Penny Candy, Bobskates

the Buick, and I decided to check it out. I had heard several hairy tales about the methods employed by used car salesmen, and I was determined not to be taken in by any smooth-talking, high-pressure sales pitch. As soon as I spotted the car on the lot, I was quite taken with it. It looked like it had been well taken care of; no dents in the body, no cracks in the windows. A young lad was painting the sidewalls of the tires black to make them look better than they really were, and I asked him what the car was selling for. He replied, "Four hundred dollars." I sensed that I was now one up on the salesman. When he came over, we talked about the car for a couple of minutes, and then, out of the blue, I offered him $375 cash. It immediately became obvious that I had outwitted him. He accepted without any argument. He recognized that he had met his match. It wasn't until two months later, when "Smiling Ben" became a sponsor at the station, that I found out the car had been on the lot at $350! So much for outsmarting a used car salesman.

That Buick was involved in a rather unusual incident about three months after I bought it and two months before it was sold for junk. The staff at the radio station had decided to have a Halloween masquerade party. I went as a tramp, and we were partying in Ted Reynold's suite in the Savoy Mansions before proceeding to the station. Someone noticed quite a commotion outside, and when I went to the window to have a look, I was stunned to see smoke pouring out of the Buick's windows. The fire had attracted a small crowd and the services of a hook and ladder truck, plus the Fire Chief. I proceeded outside and had some difficulty in convincing the Chief that the car was mine. Being dressed not unlike the winos who slept under the Johnson Street bridge, and having enjoyed a martini or two, didn't help. I eventually learned that someone had apparently flicked a firecracker through the open car window, setting the front seat ablaze. The superintendent of the Savoy Mansions had been the first to spot the fire and had pulled the apartment block alarm. When the fire department received a call to the three-storey apartment, it responded with its major equipment. As a result of all that, I got a brand new front seat courtesy of my insurance company, which turned out to be the only part of the car that was worth anything two months later.

When Doris and I chose the first week in January to get married, it wasn't the smartest thing we could have done. First of all, if we had married one week earlier, in December, I could have claimed her on my income tax for the entire year. That wasn't too serious, however, because I wasn't being paid enough to make claiming a dependent mean much. The real problem was that Christmas in a radio station is the busiest time of the year. Just about every business in the city wants to buy a Christmas greeting; a one-minute message wishing everyone happiness, good health, much success and so on, ad nauseam. By this time, I had become copy editor at the station, having decided that a career as an announcer for the next forty years was not my cup of tea. As copy editor I decided to assume responsibility for writing all of the Christmas greetings, which probably numbered close to one hundred, to free my writers for the numerous Christmas programs we had to produce. This pressure of Christmas writing (after all, how many ways are there to say "Merry Christmas?"), coupled with planning the wedding and interspersed with the inevitable last-minute Christmas shopping, took their toll.

By the time I was ready to walk down the aisle, I was too numb to be nervous. This post-Christmas syndrome may well be the reason that we got lost driving to Brentwood following our reception at Terry's Tearoom. At 11:30 that night we found ourselves in the middle of Butchart Gardens and were set to spend the night curled up in our new Morris Minor. Sanity prevailed, however, and we eventually found our honeymoon motel with a fire burning in the fireplace and hot chocolate delivered upon our arrival, as promised. The next day we headed back to Victoria to catch the Coho Ferry to Port Angeles, the first leg of our trip to Seattle, our honeymoon destination.

Our entrance into Seattle was not uneventful. We managed to hit the city limits during the 5:00 p.m. rush hour traffic and found ourselves practically alone, going into the city while four lanes of bumper-to-bumper cars seemed to come right at us as commuters headed to their homes in the outskirts. It was at that point that the turn signals shorted. The signals were little seven-inch arms that popped out of the doorframe between the two windows when you flicked the appropriate switch on the steering wheel. Unfortunately, when it shorted, they alternately kept popping out for several miles, giving the little British car the ludicrous look of a pregnant penguin striving for flight.

During the first few months of our marriage, we rented a small cabin in the Morrow Crest Autocourt on the Island Highway, six miles from Victoria. It had looked cute and adequate when we booked it in the fall, but when we moved in during the middle of a particularly cold winter, it proved to be a disaster. It was almost impossible to keep warm, and the night that the bed collapsed was the night we decided to move out. In April we moved into an older house located in Victoria West. The two-storey home had central heat, which the realtor convinced us was adequate for Victoria. Our ignorance proved to be our downfall. We had moved from the frying pan into the fire, or, more realistically, from the fridge into the deepfreeze. Heat from the coal-and-wood furnace in the basement blasted into the central register in the entrance hall. And that was as far as it got. There weren't any pipes from the furnace to any of the rooms, and the following winter, another humdinger for Victoria, you could almost see your breath in some of the rooms.

We had been warned against buying wet wood, so we bought two cords of "dryland" fir, only to find that "dryland" meant that the wood had never been in a logboom in the ocean. It did not rule out swampy land. We could almost wring water out of each piece. Frustrated by our experience with the wood, we converted the furnace with a sawdust burner and bought five units of sawdust that filled almost half the basement. Within seventy-two hours the place was crawling with fleas. I phoned the sawdust dealer and asked him if he knew that his sawdust was full of fleas. "Yeah, I know. You can't get rid of them." "Well you've made a damned good start," I replied. "You gave me about ten thousand of them!" We paid an exterminator to clear the house and had to move out for forty-eight hours.

By the time our third winter had rolled around, we had graduated from wet wood to fleas to gasco briquettes, which are a coal and oil composition compressed to the size of a small orange. These presented their own unique problems. If smoke and heat were in direct correlation, we would have been living in the equivalent of the tropics. The amount of smoke that poured from our chimney on a daily basis was the equal of a dozen burning truck tires. It is because of all these problems we had in our first house that we enshrined the heat pump in the backyard of our present home. The difference is the same as going from a skateboard to a sportscar. Viva la differance!

Our firstborn, Monte, arrived on the scene on June 24, 1952. By this time I had forsaken my career in radio to become a provincial government employee. I had become disenchanted with radio and very enchanted with

and Frozen Roadapples

Victoria, so government service seemed to offer the security I was looking for. Monte's brother, Rick, arrived on September 30, 1954, and by the time their sister, Leanne, had joined them on October 17, 1960, we were living in a much nicer house in a newer part of the city.

In order to supplement my meagre income, I enlisted in a local militia unit, the 5th (B.C.) Independent Medium Battery, Royal Regiment of Canadian Artillery. I joined as a sergeant and within three years had risen to a captaincy (a sad commentary on the standards of Canada's reserve army). The work was interesting, the money much appreciated and the camaraderie most enjoyable. The militia was not without its humorous moments, particularly in the Officers' Mess. The patron saint of artillerymen in the British Commonwealth is St. Barbara, and the annual St. Barbara's Day Dinner is the highlight of our social season. The most junior officer in the unit is tagged with making the toast to the Queen at the start of the dinner. The toast is simply, "Gentleman, the Queen. Our Captain-General." Now, the problem in making the toast is that it doesn't take place until sometime around 9 p.m. In view of the fact that you haven't eaten since lunch and you have been imbibing more than you should, the toast often turns out to be the junior officer's Waterloo. Like the evening he lurched to his feet and, with all the dignity he could muster, said: "Gentlemen, the Queen. Our Postmaster General."

I made a rule during the first year of our marriage from which we have never deviated. I make all the major decisions, and when anything goes wrong Doris takes the blame. It's worked like a charm all through the years. It holds true to this day, and I would recommend it to young couples embarking on the sea of matrimony because it is a marital philosophy that has stood the test of time. There is one other excellent guideline I would like to pass along, and that is . . . *never* go to bed mad. (I think that the longest we went without sleep was one week.)

I have done my share of housework, but when it comes to fixing things, I have to admit that I'm a few bricks short of a load. The day I "fixed" the doorway to the carport is a good example of what I mean. The frame at the top was split, and rather than wait for the board to completely break, which would definitely need a carpenter to repair, I hammered a one-and-a-half-inch finishing nail through the board. When Doris came back from shopping, her arms loaded with groceries, she tried the door and thought it was locked. "Let me in," she shouted.

Penny Candy, Bobskates

"For pete's sake, open the bloody door," I shouted.

"It won't open."

"Well, it's not locked, maybe it's stuck. Try again!" That got her Irish up. She backed across the carport, took a firm grip on the bags, and charged the door. She broke all twelve eggs and mashed six bananas. I had hammered the nail through the board and well into the door! On another occasion, I attempted to build a compost box. I couldn't get it square for the life of me and quit in frustration. Monte finished it for me. He was eleven.

One of the nice things about growing older is having grandchildren. We are fortunate that three of our grandchildren (two boys and a girl) live here in Victoria, and our other granddaughter lives on the Mainland, only a ferry ride away. In fairness to their parents, we try not to spoil them, but it isn't easy. Doris is forever knitting baby clothes when they are tiny and then sewing dresses, dressing gowns and little boy's pants and jackets as they grow. We like to be there when the kiddies are sick, or taking their first steps, or having birthday parties, and we all plan to get together at Christmas. Having raised three of our own, we try to take everything in stride, try not to be surprised at anything they do and try to remain calm during any crisis that may develop. But we do get caught off-guard at times. Like when Rick phoned to say, "We won't be over. We have to take Jess to the clinic. He stuffed cat food pellets up his nose." I guess he's just a normal four-year-old boy. Six months ago, he stuck a dried bean in his ear. We're dreading the next call.

As with most parents, our lives revolved around our children during their growing up years. When the time came for them to leave home to seek their fortune and establish their own lives, there was a part of us that didn't want to let go. We still refer to them as "the kids." I tried to express this sentiment in the following, which was written for my daughter Leanne. It was first published in Victoria's *Times-Colonist* in September, 1982. It was also recorded with a musical background by Barry Bowman for his "Morning Mayor" program on CFAX, Victoria. It's called . . .

Daddy's Little Girl

My little girl entered a new world yesterday . . . it was her first day of school. She seems so tiny, so vulnerable to have to cope all by herself. It is as though a chapter on the innocence of childhood has been closed and she is suddenly thrust into a world of give and take, a world that is both

166

and Frozen Roadapples

strange and frightening, where she will often feel alone and lonely.

Mommy is no longer there to cuddle her when she's frightened . . . kiss the pain away when she's hurt . . . assure her when she's uncertain. So, first of all world, help her to realize that her teacher also loves her, even if it's just a little bit, and that all the other kids have the same mixed feelings of excitement and fear, timidity and false bravado.

And after she has settled in and feels more comfortable, let her learn that it is not necessary to be teacher's pet, nor is it popular to be a class cut-up. Rather, help her to appreciate and respect those who are trying to make her a better person. And, please world, don't let my little girl be the one who laughs at the child on crutches, or teases a classmate who speaks funny, or whose skin is coloured or whose eyes are shaped differently. Help her to know that we are all God's creatures, each with a spot to fill and a reason for being. Let her heart go out to those less fortunate.

And as she enters her teens, give her strength to ignore the pressures of her peers, and the courage to stand up against that which she knows to be wrong. And if she is not pretty enough to be a class beauty, or personable enough to be a cheerleader, or smart enough to be an honour student, please help her to accept that which cannot be changed, and help her to realize that beauty from within is far more important and more lasting than that which is without.

Teach her to have respect and pride. And when the time comes, as it may, that she wants to share herself with someone who professes to love her, let her recognize the difference between love and infatuation, between sincerity and deceit.

Teach her to be gentle but strong . . . charitable but selective . . . loving but independent . . . tolerant but principled.

Teach her not to take life too seriously, to keep all things in perspective, and to learn to laugh at herself and with others. Let her always be lady-like, feminine and affectionate . . . to always love puppies, kittens, frilly clothes, dolls and above all, children. For one day she will marry and, God willing, she will share in the miracle of birth. And then, and only then, will she know the profound pleasure, the anxieties and concerns, and the unbounded pride, that are common to all parents.

And, world, when that day comes, and she finds a new man in her life, someone whom she loves with all her heart, please give me the strength to let go, for that will surely be one of the most difficult things I will have to do . . . because she will always be 'Daddy's little girl.'

Afterthoughts

One of the first chores foisted on a prairie lad was the removal of ashes from the ashpit in the furnace and lugging them by the pailful to the ashpile beside the lane. It was a daily chore. The size of some of the cinders always amazed me; they were like large chunks of lava. I guess in a way, that is what they were. Each week a city truck came down the back lanes, and the ashpiles were taken away.

The coldest day I ever remember was during the winter of 1942-43 when I was going to university. The radio said that Saskatoon's temperature was sixty degrees below zero, "the coldest spot in Canada and an all-time record." I had an early morning class, and I remember hauling Dad's old buffalo coat out of the closet and putting it on. I was reasonably comfortable, but it was only a three-quarter-length coat, and my legs were awfully cold. You couldn't walk quickly because the cold air cut your lungs like a knife. Some of the streetcars developed "black rail" and were unable to move. The problem came about because the wheels would spin on the iced rail, the friction melted the ice, the cold air refroze the water and the cycle went on and on, making the rail black. The streetcar couldn't move an inch.

I wonder what ever happened to "pinkeye"? Maybe it is still around and I just don't hear about it. It was a weird kind of eye infection, and sixty years ago, no one seemed to know what caused it or how to cure it. There seemed to be a season for pinkeye, and once it was over with, you

168

and Frozen Roadapples

didn't have to worry about catching it for another year. Parents used to warn their children about looking into the eyes of anyone who had it because that is the way they thought it was spread from one kid to another. If you woke up one morning with one or both eyes quite pink and sore looking, you could count on a strange week with your friends. They would play with you, but they wouldn't look you in the eye.

I always found it interesting as I grew up to observe the occupations chosen by the city's various ethnic groups. Fifty years ago, most of the restaurants were operated by Greeks (Spiros Leakos was a neighbour of ours for a while); the laundries were nearly all Chinese; fruit and vegetable dealers, especially the door-to-door pedlars, were Italian, and many of the clothing stores were Jewish.

I wonder if youngsters still play the string game that used to fascinate us? All you needed was a piece of string approximately twenty-four inches long. You tied the ends together and then placed the looped string over your hands, which were held facing each other, holding the string taut. You then proceeded to make various designs by threading the string through your fingers, pulling the string tight after each manoeuvre. Some got very clever at making intricate designs or patterns. Others never seemed to be able to master the game.

Every boy had a collection of glass marbles, which he carried in a small bag with a drawstring top. Some were solid colours and others had multi-coloured swirls. The most popular were the "cat's eyes," which could get you three for one in a trade. You also had a favourite "shooter," which was traded only when its luck at winning had run out. A popular game with marbles was made out of a small box, preferably a shoe box. Doorways of varying sizes, from very small to very large, were cut in the box. Over the smallest opening would be the number "10," and over the largest, the number "2." This meant that you would give ten marbles to anyone who could roll their marble through that door from a distance of about six feet and two marbles for the easier entrance. Other numbers were placed over the remaining doors, consistent with the degree of difficulty. It was a lot of fun, and boxes would be set up at recess like a bunch of little gambling concessions . . . which is what they were.

Labour Day was an exciting time when you were a youngster in school. It was also called Arbour Day, and it was the day when students in the city's public schools were each given a seedling, usually pine, to plant in their

169

yard at home. When I left home some fifteen years later, my seedling had grown into a majestic tree of some twenty feet in height. I'd wager that to this day, there are some backyards in Saskatoon graced by fifty-foot pines which were planted by some enthused youngster in the 1930's.

In our neighbourhood, potato roasts were almost as popular as wiener roasts. We usually had ours in a neighbour's garden in the fall when their potatoes were mature. We would dig a shallow trench, fill it with potatoes, cover them with rocks and then build a fire on the rocks. In about an hour you removed the ashes and rocks, and the potatoes would be roasted to perfection. You stuck your potato on a popsicle stick, peeled it and ate it with butter and salt. Delicious!

Publication of Nutana Collegiate's yearbook, *The Hermes*, was always looked forward to with a great deal of excitement at the end of each school year. Photographs of school activities, of each class, and of individual students in their senior years, were interesting, and the comments made beside your photograph were sometimes flattering, but not always. Little did we realize at the time how much we would cherish each yearbook twenty, thirty, forty years and more down the road. The memories they evoke are invaluable.

Popular portrait photographers that I recall from those days were Charmbury's, Henry Thams and Gibson's studios. The most prominent freelance photographer was little Len Hillyard, whose photos of major events in Saskatoon cover several decades and will provide future generations with a valuable pictoral history.

Stew Parr's dad owned Parr's Men's Clothing, and in the basement of their house there were several bottles of showcard paint that he used for making advertising posters for the store windows. One afternoon Stew and I decided it would be a good idea to paint our shoes different colours. We proceeded to paint the toecaps orange, the heels red, one side green and the other white. The finished product was really kind of neat. A little garish, but real cool. We wore them to collegiate for three or four days, but Mr. Bonney, the principal, said that they were "distracting" to classmates and suggested we didn't wear them.

A teenage pastime that didn't cost anything was to go to a music store and listen to new recordings on the pretext that you were in the market to purchase one or two. The stores had individual booths, and two or three chums could cram in together and listen to new recordings for up

and Frozen Roadapples

to an hour. It was an abuse that stores soon put a lid on by restricting it to one person per booth for a maximum of thirty minutes with the provision that you buy at least one record. In a couple of years, stores eliminated the booths entirely.

One summer, a year or two after the war, and at a time I was in Saskatoon between radio jobs, I bumped into Erwin Schellenberg on 2nd Avenue. Erwin's family had moved to Kelowna in 1940 where his father retired and bought a small orchard named "Belgo House." The orchard was six to ten acres in size and had its own lake for boating and swimming. During this particular period, a time when the used car market was quite lucrative, Erwin came to Saskatoon once a week by train, bought a used car, drove it back to Kelowna by way of the Big Bend Highway and made himself a couple of hundred dollars a week. He had just purchased a convertible, and when he found out that I was at loose ends, he invited me to go back with him and spend a week on the orchard. Erwin and I had been friends since grade 1 at Victoria School, and I was only too pleased to accept. We left within the hour.

The trip through the Big Bend was interesting, to say the least. We were driving through the mountains in the middle of the night, heading for our overnight stay in Golden, when we were deluged by a terrific rainstorm. It was at this point we learned that the car's windshield wipers didn't function. It was not the best of news, but we were grateful that the convertible's roof worked. Erwin had made the trip several times, and he knew that when a sign said "Slow to 30," he could take it quite comfortably at forty. I didn't have the luxury of that knowledge. Erwin's high-speed driving, combined with the fact that we had our noses pressed against the windshield in an effort to keep the highway in view, made the trip somewhat less than relaxing. By the time we got to Golden, my right leg should have been twice its normal size from slamming on the brakes in a knee-jerk reaction. Good driving, and a bit of luck, got us to Kelowna in one piece, and I thoroughly enjoyed my week at Belgo House. Mr. Schellenberg took considerable pleasure in showing me his successful experimentation in dehydrating peaches, cherries, plums and other fruits grown on his orchard. Erwin's older brother, Dave, and his wife had a party for us at their home, and we somehow glommed onto a trio that had been performing at the Yacht Club. We soon found that amplified

Penny Candy, Bobskates

electronic drums, a guitar and accordion played in a small room can have quite a sobering effect. Like holding a rock concert in a broom closet.

It was some years later when tragedy struck the Schellenberg family. Their youngest, sixteen-year-old Harry, had taken a shotgun and, wearing inflatable hip waders, the type with the inner tube attached, had gone out into the lake. He was out of sight of the house when he apparently snagged the waders on an underwater obstacle. The ruptured waders filled with water, and the young lad drowned.

When I worked at CJVI, I used to chum around with some of the reporters from the two local newspapers, the *Times* and the *Colonist*. (In recent years the two papers have amalgamated.) Johnny ''Pinhead'' McLean was a reporter/photographer at the *Colonist* who achieved journalistic prominence in later years at the *Toronto Telegram*. In one of his exploits, he somehow managed to stow away on board *HMCS Magnificent*, Canada's only aircraft carrier, and on another occasion, he was the only reporter to get inside Kingston Penitentiary during a riot. He got his hands on a fireman's outfit (he never explained how) and went into the prison with other firemen to help put out a fire started by the inmates.

I got involved in one of his milder escapades during the winter of 1949-50. Victoria, which fronts the Strait of Juan de Fuca, is subjected to some pretty nasty storms that sweep in from the Pacific Ocean. As a matter of fact, many years ago, the crashing of waves spawned by a major storm dislodged a casket from one of the city's oldest cemeteries located in Ross Bay and swept it out to sea. In January of the year in question, we were having a dandy mid-winter storm with winds gusting to over eighty knots and waves exceeding ten feet in height. Our seafront roadway, Dallas Road, had been closed to traffic in the Ross Bay area, and Johnny talked me into driving my '29 Buick around the barriers and parking the car in the middle of the prohibited stretch of road. He wanted to get a photograph of a huge wave coming directly at us, breaking over the car. He managed, with great difficulty, to climb onto the roof of the car, and then he instructed me to hold his ankles. I was not only afraid that I might very well drown in the middle of a road in the middle of the afternoon, but it also occurred to me that anyone witnessing this exhibition would have every right to try to get us committed. In a matter of seconds, a big wave crashed over the seawall, pinned me against the car and threw Johnny backwards with me holding onto his ankles for dear life. The net result

and Frozen Roadapples

was two sprained ankles, a waterlogged camera and two people who should have known better soaked to the "nines." I still have a terrific photo that he took of the storm from a safer vantage point with a second camera. Johnny passed away a few years ago, and news reports in Eastern papers called him "the last of the old time reporters."

Living in boarding houses was an interesting experience. Like people, they came in all shapes and sizes, and each had its own personality. When I was single, I lived in seven different boarding homes in four different cities . . . one in Winnipeg, two in Regina, two in Kamloops and two in Victoria. The worst, and the best were in Regina. The former was a small bungalow owned by an older couple who were within months of retirement. He was a chicken plucker (I kid you not) in a local poultry firm. I was their first boarder. The meals were skimpy and sort of weird. The fanciest Sunday dinner served in the two months of my stay was stuffed beef heart. Whenever I was to be alone in the house, the landlady went down to the basement and disconnected the phone "so that you can't run up any long distance bills!" It was somewhat less than a nice, friendly atmosphere.

My next move was to a boarding home on Scarth Street, opposite Central Collegiate. It was a three-storey brick house with twelve boarders. And get this: the landlady was single and twenty-five years of age! Every Saturday night was PARTY TIME! A rather humorous (except to me) incident took place one weekend when weird circumstances ganged up to rob me of a new pair of shoes. Here's what happened. Early Saturday afternoon I had purchased a new pair of leather dress shoes. When I got home, I placed them under the bed in readiness for the evening wingding. The landlady came in to vacuum the room and placed my shoes in the metal wastebasket to get them out of the way. My roomie returned from an afternoon of guzzling beer. His stomach, offended by the abuse of its owner, rebelled. He dashed for the only bathroom in the house. As was usually the case, it was occupied. He bolted back to the bedroom, grabbed the wastebasket, and threw up. End of shoes.

The only rooming house I ever stayed in was in Benito, Manitoba, in 1947 when I was trying to sell sets of encyclopedia, mostly in homes where only Ukrainian was spoken. The one set I almost sold was to a widow with four children who told me that she would spend the money she set aside for a bicycle to buy a set of books. I told her to buy the bike. My "sales

173

Penny Candy, Bobskates

career'' lasted four days. There was no hotel at that time, so I rented a room with a Russian family, located above a grocery store. A large picture of Lenin dominated the livingroom, and the elderly grandfather wore bib overalls twenty-four hours a day. The bedrooms were separated by walls of corrugated cardboard, and the chemical toilet for the ten residents was located inches from the head of my bed. It was an interesting two nights.

In the summer of 1950, an event of some significance took place in Esquimalt Harbour with the arrival of the flagship of the British East India's Fleet under the command of an admiral whose name escapes me. A press conference was laid on to meet the admiral, and Ted Reynolds and I were chosen to represent CJVI. I wasn't on the newsroom staff and couldn't understand why I was chosen. The press party of approximately ten journalists assembled on board the flagship and were met by the ship's press officer, a young lt. commander. We introduced ourselves and then followed him down to the Admiral's wardroom. The Press Officer proceeded to introduce each of us by name and designated who we represented. A phenomenal feat of memory. I possibly appreciated this more than most because I have considerable difficulty remembering names to the point that I have been going to introduce my wife and have drawn a blank. Here was a chap who met ten total strangers and several minutes later introduced each one without missing a beat.

The admiral asked us to be seated, but because we thought it only proper that the admiral be the first to sit down, and he in turn quite properly fully expected his guests to be seated first, it became a Mexican standoff, and we all remained standing for the entire press conference. It was an omen of things to come. The admiral graciously passed a sterling cigarette box around, and we each took one. I didn't smoke, but I had seen enough movies to know that reporters always smoke. The press officer lit each cigarette, and the interview began. I had a notebook in my left hand and a pen in my right, so the cigarette remained in the corner of my mouth with the smoke curling up into my right eye. For some reason I felt like Humphrey Bogart, but I probably looked like Mickey Rooney. I am sure the admiral was impressed. We took turns asking questions, and the only one I could think of when it was my turn was, "What do you think of the European situation?" It was brief, to the point and, I thought, relevant. Ted started to laugh and made out that he was choking from the cigarette

174

smoke. Things were not improving. In the middle of questions from the media reps, Johnny McLean said, "Excuse me, admiral, but I want to get a photo. Would you be good enough to pose beside that stuffed crow?" Johnny had no way of knowing that the admiral was a respected ornithologist with an international reputation and that the "crow" was a very rare species from the heart of the Belgian Congo. The press conference had bottomed out. The press officer explained the bird's origins, the admiral posed for a photo and the questions were brought to an end. We all left. The admiral took early retirement.

I think that the press conference also took its toll on me because within a few months, I decided to leave broadcasting and seek a career in the public service.

Twenty-eight years later I retired as Director of Information Services with the Provincial Ministry of Health. I hasten to add that I was not a political appointee, as was the case with many of the senior positions in Information Services. Rather I had worked my way up from the trenches. My career had been both interesting and frustrating (government service has more than its share of the latter). In my last position I was responsible for writing the minister's major addresses (thirteen in one four-month period, many with two days' notice); arranging press conferences; writing press releases; developing pamphlets; serving as editor of the ministry's annual report; organizing the "official opening" of new hospitals and institutions and so on. All with the help of two former journalists as staff members. In 1975, when I lost a good friend from lung cancer induced by years of smoking cigarettes, I originated, researched and developed an anti-smoking pamphlet. The timing was right as we became among the first in the "kick-the-habit" movement, and the minister made it a major project by promoting the pamphlet through the legislature. (In so doing, my name became part of the Hansard, a privilege accorded few public servants.) Eventually, approximately 300,000 copies found their way throughout the province, across Canada and into the States. A New York insurance carrier requested, and received, permission to reproduce the pamphlet. I have a file folder full of copies of letters from people who wrote to say that the pamphlet had helped them kick their habit. Some had smoked two packs a day for thirty years. It is a nice feeling to know that you may have been instrumental in helping someone avoid the nightmare of cancer.

Penny Candy, Bobskates

Revisiting Old Friends and Old Haunts

Doris and I had planned to visit Saskatoon in the middle of September, 1987, preceded by a visit to the West Edmonton Mall. However, the late arrival of our newest grandchild delayed our trip until the first week of October. Grandmother wanted to be available to baby-sit Rick and Debbie's two other children and had been busy for many weeks making a comforter for the crib and knitting baby clothes. Kayla Morgan Thompson arrived September 20 and looked surprisingly like our daughter's little girl, Amber.

Both Doris and I had fond memories of travelling by train many years ago, so we booked a bedroom on VIA Rail from Vancouver to Edmonton for a three-day stay and then on to Saskatoon by coach. We soon found that many things had changed since our last train trip. For one thing, there is no longer any "clickety clack," or "ding, ding, ding." The former, made by the steel wheels bumping over joins in the track, was eliminated with the new method of laying continuous ribbons of steel, mile after mile. The latter sound was made by the clanging of the bell at every crossing that had an automatic barrier. With the encroachment of housing developments at the majority of train crossings, residents complained about the disquieting clamour of tolling bells, and most of them were removed. Meals in the dining car were excellent, with reserved seatings at 5:45, 6:45 and 8:00 p.m. The last was the only one at which

and Frozen Roadapples

smoking was permitted. Surprisingly enough, our sleeping car attendant was a young lady from Vancouver who had been with VIA Rail for seven years. Gone are the days of the "coloured" porter and the overnight shoeshine. The lounge car, which served drinks, was one-half of the dining car, with limited seating for about sixteen customers. To our disappointment, there was no dome car on our train. Our sleeping car was the last of a ten-car train, and as a result, we kept sliding around in our berths from the whiplash effect caused by the train taking curves at relatively high speeds. It made sleeping a little difficult, but it was certainly different. Everything considered, we quite enjoyed the train.

The first day at Edmonton was reserved for a reunion with my boyhood chum, John Schmitz, whom I had last seen in 1963. The second day was spent at the Mall, and the third was used for sightseeing. John had transferred to Edmonton with Imperial Oil in the 1960's and was now retired. Doris and I spent the afternoon and evening with John, his wife, Florence and their two daughters, Jan and Barbara. I had a photograph with me that was taken sixty-two years ago. It was of John, his brother, Jim, and myself, all holding hands; and in the background were his sisters, Irma, Margaret and Rita, and my sister, Pat. We were dressed in our Sunday best — my outfit looked like a dress! (Jim had passed away a few years previously.)

The next day John and I were both hoarse from a marathon of talking, recalling things we had done more than half a century ago. He had read my original manuscript and was dumbfounded that he could not recall the incident when his dad got a fish hook through his thumbnail. He reminded me of neighbours whom I had forgotten, including the Lepers, and Grant and Kay Fletcher, brothers who lived in the 400 block on 9th Street. At the mention of their names, I remembered having seen the teenaged brothers playing a game of horseshoes in their backyard that ended in what could have been a serious injury. Grant had thrown his second shoe and was walking towards the other pit when Kay's last shoe caught on the ring of his index finger. It sent the shoe awry, hitting Grant on the shoulder. The broken ring dug deeply into Kay's finger and had to be removed with pliers. The whole episode was quite exciting for someone who was just six years old. Grant was killed during the war and is one of the names I had forgotten from the list of Nutana Collegiate students who made the supreme sacrifice.

Penny Candy, Bobskates

Our day at the West Edmonton Mall was very interesting but probably a little disappointing because of the excessive media coverage it had received when it opened. We expected to see Disneyland in the middle of the Ala Moana Shopping Centre. Doris and I rented the individual, battery-operated carts that are available and rode through the Mall and Fantasyland for four hours, thoroughly enjoying this relaxed method of sightseeing. We were among the first on Monday morning to use the carts, and every Japanese tourist who passed us took our photo, most of them with camcorders. If we ever get to Japan, we should be fairly well known.

Our seven-hour trip by train to Saskatoon was quite interesting until it got dark, then the last three hours were somewhat boring. We arrived at 11:45 p.m. I had sent a copy of my book to Herb Pinder, and he was kind enough to write and say that he found it "not just interesting, but fascinating." Herb and I hadn't seen each other for more than forty years. I was his guest at the Saskatoon Club where we reminisced for two hours over lunch. Gordie Bowman, who had read Herb's copy of the book, was unable to join us because he was leaving that morning to visit his daughter in Winnipeg. In Gordie's letter, written in response to the book, he said, "I found it so interesting I couldn't put it down until I was finished." These compliments were very flattering, but what was most pleasing was that the book could provide so much pleasure. He recalled a theatre that I had overlooked: the Bijou, later known as the Ritz, next to the Ritz Hotel between 1st and 2nd Avenues. Felix the Cat and Oswald the Lucky Rabbit were cartoons he remembered enjoying.

Both Herb and Gordie mentioned Dever's Confectionary, kitty-corner from Victoria School. Mr. Dever reminded Herb of Andy Gump. The store was next to Dyke's Service Station, whose owners both wore bow ties and, according to Gordie, looked like Mutt and Jeff. (Who says kids aren't influenced by comic strips?) Herb also confirmed something that Phyllis Harrington had caught: the Swiss Village and Mountain project was in grade 3, not in grade 2. They also reminded me that the bowling alley I wrote about was Fingard's on 3rd Avenue, between 22nd and 23rd Streets. Still a mystery, however, is the bowling alley of only five lanes on the second floor of some downtown building. We played our first game of "5 Pin" there in the early '30s.

Doris and I stayed with my sister, Pat, who took us on numerous drives throughout the city. The houses of several childhood friends still

178

remained, and each held special memories. We visited the Western Development Museum, which is excellent. A walk down the old-time street is a walk down memory lane. Unfortunately, with the exception of a few buildings and a few houses, the hometown of my childhood no longer exists.

Pat recalled that when she and her teenaged friends holidayed at Manitou Lake, Watrous, in the late 1920's and early 1930's, the Guy Watkins band played for dances. Guy was a blind musician. In my teenaged years, Saskatoon's most popular dance band was led by Ken Peaker and featured one or two of his brothers. A couple of years ago I had a chat with Ken when he was playing the piano for guests in one of Victoria's popular dining lounges.

Saskatoon has grown from 30,000 to a thriving 182,000. The CN Railyards, the 20th Street overpass and the cenotaph, are gone. The Capitol and Daylight theatres have fallen to the wrecker's ball. The campus of the university, at one time "comfortable" to be on, now is sprawling. The city is criss-crossed with freeways, and its skyline has changed dramatically. The riverbank is now landscaped, and the trees of our youth have fallen to the chainsaw. And all that is as it should be. To be otherwise would suggest that the city fathers lacked foresight and that Saskatonians lacked industry, neither of which would be correct.

Revisiting your former home is like being in the presence of a dear and very old friend who can no longer speak. Your communication is with your eyes and your heart. Here is where you grew from childhood to manhood; where you were loved, fed and clothed, cared for when you were sick and taught some of life's disciplines. That is why it is sad to find that your home of sixty years ago has made way for an apartment block.

The houses of your childhood may be torn down; the playgrounds you played on may be covered with highrises; and your favourite school "hangouts" and cafes may no longer exist. But the memories remain. To relive them, you need only shut your eyes.

As I reflect on what life was like sixty years ago, the obvious comparisons with today are nothing less than incredible. In the 1930's our houses didn't have oil heat, fibreglass insulation, thermopane windows, air conditioning, smoke alarms, automatic dishwashers, electric blenders or microwave ovens. Business offices didn't have computers, photocopiers, intercom systems, electric typewriters or fax machines.

Penny Candy, Bobskates

Automobiles didn't have fuel injected engines, power steering and power brakes, heaters, or cruise control. Doctors didn't perform bypass surgery, transplant organs, implant embryos, do CAT scans, or provide shots for polio and influenza. Farmers worked their fields with cultivators, seeders, harrows, and combines, all powered by horses. In the 1930's we didn't smoke grass, we mowed it. We didn't shoot coke, we drank it. Couples didn't live together, then marry, for awhile; we married, and then lived together, forever. My generation grew up through a depression and fought in a war. We met the challenges of the times head on. We were achievers then. We are survivors now.

Who could ask for more?

Epilogue

It seems to me that as we enter the winter of our lives, we cherish more and more those places and those friends associated with our springtime. With each advancing year we recognize the fragility of the thread that holds us, and we feel blessed for the privilege of being a survivor. Rapport with friends not seen for decades seems immediate. For there is a bond . . . and that bond is time.

This book of boyhood memories has been a labour of love, with a reward beyond all expectations because of the pleasure it has brought to so many.

The names, dates and events are as I remember them. In those instances where my memory is shown to be faulty, I hope that I will be forgiven.

I would be delighted to hear from you. Please write to me at:

1691 Stanhope Place
Victoria, B.C.
V8P 1Y2

Bob Thompson lived in Saskatoon from 1925 to 1947. He moved to Victoria in 1948, where he and Doris, his wife of thirty-nine years, live in retirement. His hobbies are writing, walking, travelling, and "keeping track of his grandchildren."